WILLIAM SHAKESPEARE was born in Stratford-upon-Avon in April, 1564, and his birth is traditionally celebrated on April 23. The facts of his life, known from surviving documents, are sparse. He was one of eight children born to John Shakespeare, a merchant of some standing in his community. William probably went to the King's New School in Stratford, but he had no university education. In November 1582, at the age of eighteen, he married Anne Hathaway, eight years his senior, who was pregnant with their first child, Susanna. She was born on May 26, 1583. Twins, a boy, Hamnet (who would die at age eleven), and a girl, Judith, were born in 1585. By 1592 Shakespeare had gone to London, working as an actor and already known as a playwright. A rival dramatist, Robert Greene, referred to him as "an upstart crow, beautified with our feathers." Shakespeare became a principal shareholder and playwright of the successful acting troupe the Lord Chamberlain's men (later, under James I, called the King's men). In 1599 the Lord Chamberlain's men built and occupied the Globe Theatre in Southwark near the Thames River. Here many of Shakespeare's plays were performed by the most famous actors of his time, including Richard Burbage, Will Kempe, and Robert Armin. In addition to his 37 plays, Shakespeare had a hand in others, including *Sir Thomas More* and *The Two Noble Kinsmen,* and he wrote poems, including *Venus and Adonis* and *The Rape of Lucrece.* His 154 sonnets were published, probably without his authorization, in 1609. In 1611 or 1612 he gave up his lodgings in London and devoted more and more of his time to retirement in Stratford, though he continued writing such plays as *The Tempest* and *Henry VIII* until about 1613. He died on April 23, 1616, and was buried in Holy Trinity Church, Stratford. No collected edition of his plays was published during his lifetime, but in 1623 two members of his acting company, John Heminges and Henry Condell, published the great collection now called the First Folio.

Bantam Shakespeare
The Complete Works—29 Volumes
Edited by David Bevington
With forewords by Joseph Papp on the plays

The Poems: Venus and Adonis, The Rape of Lucrece, The
Phoenix and Turtle, A Lover's Complaint,
the Sonnets

Antony and Cleopatra	*The Merchant of Venice*
As You Like It	*A Midsummer Night's Dream*
The Comedy of Errors	*Much Ado about Nothing*
Hamlet	*Othello*
Henry IV, Part One	*Richard II*
Henry IV, Part Two	*Richard III*
Henry V	*Romeo and Juliet*
Julius Caesar	*The Taming of the Shrew*
King Lear	*The Tempest*
Macbeth	*Twelfth Night*

Together in one volume:

Henry VI, Parts One, Two, and Three
King John and Henry VIII
Measure for Measure, All's Well that Ends Well, and
Troilus and Cressida
Three Early Comedies: Love's Labor's Lost, The Two
Gentlemen of Verona, The Merry
Wives of Windsor
Three Classical Tragedies: Titus Andronicus, Timon
of Athens, Coriolanus
The Late Romances: Pericles, Cymbeline, The Winter's
Tale, The Tempest

Two collections:

Four Comedies: The Taming of the Shrew, A Midsummer
Night's Dream, The Merchant of Venice,
Twelfth Night
Four Tragedies: Hamlet, Othello, King Lear, Macbeth

William Shakespeare

MUCH ADO ABOUT NOTHING

Edited by
David Bevington

David Scott Kastan,
James Hammersmith,
and Robert Kean Turner,
Associate Editors

With a Foreword by
Joseph Papp

BANTAM BOOKS
TORONTO / NEW YORK / LONDON / SYDNEY / AUCKLAND

MUCH ADO ABOUT NOTHING
*A Bantam Book / published by arrangement
with Scott, Foresman and Company*

PRINTING HISTORY
*Scott, Foresman edition published / January 1980
Bantam edition, with newly edited text and substantially revised, edited,
and amplified notes, introductions, and other
materials, published / February 1988
Valuable advice on staging matters has been
provided by Richard Hosley.
Collations checked by Eric Rasmussen.
Additional editorial assistance by Claire McEachern.*

Library of Congress Cataloging-in-Publication Data

Shakespeare, William, 1564–1616.
   Much ado about nothing / William Shakespeare; edited by David
Bevington; David Scott Kastan, James Hammersmith, and Robert Kean
Turner, associate editors; with a foreword by Joseph Papp.
      p.   cm.—(A Bantam classic)
   "Bantam edition with newly edited text and substantially revised,
edited, and amplified notes, introductions, and other materials"—
—T.p. verso.
   Bibliography: p.
   ISBN 0-553-21301-6 (pbk.)
   I. Bevington, David M.   II. Title.
PR2828.A2B44   1988
822.3'3—dc19   87–23200
                                                                        CIP

Published simultaneously in the United States and Canada

PRINTED IN THE UNITED STATES OF AMERICA

O   0 9 8 7 6 5 4 3 2 1

Contents

Foreword

It's hard to imagine, but Shakespeare wrote all of his plays with a quill pen, a goose feather whose hard end had to be sharpened frequently. How many times did he scrape the dull end to a point with his knife, dip it into the inkwell, and bring up, dripping wet, those wonderful words and ideas that are known all over the world?

In the age of word processors, typewriters, and ballpoint pens, we have almost forgotten the meaning of the word "blot." Yet when I went to school, in the 1930s, my classmates and I knew all too well what an inkblot from the metal-tipped pens we used would do to a nice clean page of a test paper, and we groaned whenever a splotch fell across the sheet. Most of us finished the school day with ink-stained fingers; those who were less careful also went home with ink-stained shirts, which were almost impossible to get clean.

When I think about how long it took me to write the simplest composition with a metal-tipped pen and ink, I can only marvel at how many plays Shakespeare scratched out with his goose-feather quill pen, year after year. Imagine him walking down one of the narrow cobblestoned streets of London, or perhaps drinking a pint of beer in his local alehouse. Suddenly his mind catches fire with an idea, or a sentence, or a previously elusive phrase. He is burning with impatience to write it down—but because he doesn't have a ballpoint pen or even a pencil in his pocket, he has to keep the idea in his head until he can get to his quill and parchment.

He rushes back to his lodgings on Silver Street, ignoring the vendors hawking brooms, the coaches clattering by, the piteous wails of beggars and prisoners. Bounding up the stairs, he snatches his quill and starts to write furiously, not even bothering to light a candle against the dusk. "To be, or not to be," he scrawls, "that is the—." But the quill point has gone dull, the letters have fattened out illegibly, and in the middle of writing one of the most famous passages in the history of dramatic literature, Shakespeare has to stop to sharpen his pen.

Taking a deep breath, he lights a candle now that it's dark, sits down, and begins again. By the time the candle has burned out and the noisy apprentices of his French Huguenot landlord have quieted down, Shakespeare has finished Act 3 of *Hamlet* with scarcely a blot.

Early the next morning, he hurries through the fog of a London summer morning to the rooms of his colleague Richard Burbage, the actor for whom the role of Hamlet is being written. He finds Burbage asleep and snoring loudly, sprawled across his straw mattress. Not only had the actor performed in *Henry V* the previous afternoon, but he had then gone out carousing all night with some friends who had come to the performance.

Shakespeare shakes his friend awake, until, bleary-eyed, Burbage sits up in his bed. "Dammit, Will," he grumbles, "can't you let an honest man sleep?" But the playwright, his eyes shining and the words tumbling out of his mouth, says, "Shut up and listen—tell me what you think of *this*!"

He begins to read to the still half-asleep Burbage, pacing around the room as he speaks. ". . . Whether 'tis nobler in the mind to suffer the slings and arrows of outrageous fortune—"

Burbage interrupts, suddenly wide awake, "That's excellent, very good, 'the slings and arrows of outrageous fortune,' yes, I think it will work quite well. . . ." He takes the parchment from Shakespeare and murmurs the lines to himself, slowly at first but with growing excitement.

The sun is just coming up, and the words of one of Shakespeare's most famous soliloquies are being uttered for the first time by the first actor ever to bring Hamlet to life. It must have been an exhilarating moment.

Shakespeare wrote most of his plays to be performed live by the actor Richard Burbage and the rest of the Lord Chamberlain's men (later the King's men). Today, however, our first encounter with the plays is usually in the form of the printed word. And there is no question that reading Shakespeare for the first time isn't easy. His plays aren't comic books or magazines or the dime-store detective novels I read when I was young. A lot of his sentences are complex. Many of his words are no longer used in our everyday speech. His profound thoughts are often condensed into poetry, which is not as straightforward as prose.

Yet when you hear the words spoken aloud, a lot of the language may strike you as unexpectedly modern. For Shakespeare's plays, like any dramatic work, weren't really meant to be read; they were meant to be spoken, seen, and performed. It's amazing how lines that are so troublesome in print can flow so naturally and easily when spoken.

I think it was precisely this music that first fascinated me. When I was growing up, Shakespeare was a stranger to me. I had no particular interest in him, for I was from a different cultural tradition. It never occurred to me that his plays might be more than just something to "get through" in school, like science or math or the physical education requirement we had to fulfill. My passions then were movies, radio, and vaudeville—certainly not Elizabethan drama.

I was, however, fascinated by words and language. Because I grew up in a home where Yiddish was spoken, and English was only a second language, I was acutely sensitive to the musical sounds of different languages and had an ear for lilt and cadence and rhythm in the spoken word. And so I loved reciting poems and speeches even as a very young child. In first grade I learned lots of short nature verses— "Who has seen the wind?," one of them began. My first foray into drama was playing the role of Scrooge in Charles Dickens's *A Christmas Carol* when I was eight years old. I liked summoning all the scorn and coldness I possessed and putting them into the words, "Bah, humbug!"

From there I moved on to longer and more famous poems and other works by writers of the 1930s. Then, in junior high school, I made my first acquaintance with Shakespeare through his play *Julius Caesar*. Our teacher, Miss McKay, assigned the class a passage to memorize from the opening scene of the play, the one that begins "Wherefore rejoice? What conquest brings he home?" The passage seemed so wonderfully theatrical and alive to me, and the experience of memorizing and reciting it was so much fun, that I went on to memorize another speech from the play on my own.

I chose Mark Antony's address to the crowd in Act 3,

scene 2, which struck me then as incredibly high drama. Even today, when I speak the words, I feel the same thrill I did that first time. There is the strong and athletic Antony descending from the raised pulpit where he has been speaking, right into the midst of a crowded Roman square. Holding the torn and bloody cloak of the murdered Julius Caesar in his hand, he begins to speak to the people of Rome:

If you have tears, prepare to shed them now.
You all do know this mantle. I remember
The first time ever Caesar put it on;
'Twas on a summer's evening in his tent,
That day he overcame the Nervii.
Look, in this place ran Cassius' dagger through.
See what a rent the envious Casca made.
Through this the well-belovèd Brutus stabbed,
And as he plucked his cursèd steel away,
Mark how the blood of Caesar followed it,
As rushing out of doors to be resolved
If Brutus so unkindly knocked or no;
For Brutus, as you know, was Caesar's angel.
Judge, O you gods, how dearly Caesar loved him!
This was the most unkindest cut of all . . .

I'm not sure now that I even knew Shakespeare had written a lot of other plays, or that he was considered "timeless," "universal," or "classic"—but I knew a good speech when I heard one, and I found the splendid rhythms of Antony's rhetoric as exciting as anything I'd ever come across.

Fifty years later, I still feel that way. Hearing good actors speak Shakespeare gracefully and naturally is a wonderful experience, unlike any other I know. There's a satisfying fullness to the spoken word that the printed page just can't convey. This is why seeing the plays of Shakespeare performed live in a theater is the best way to appreciate them. If you can't do that, listening to sound recordings or watching film versions of the plays is the next best thing.

But if you do start with the printed word, use the play as a script. Be an actor yourself and say the lines out loud. Don't worry too much at first about words you don't immediately understand. Look them up in the footnotes or a dictionary, but don't spend too much time on this. It is more profitable (and fun) to get the sense of a passage and sing it out. Speak naturally, almost as if you were talking to a friend, but be sure to enunciate the words properly. You'll be surprised at how much you understand simply by speaking the speech "trippingly on the tongue," as Hamlet advises the Players.

You might start, as I once did, with a speech from *Julius Caesar*, in which the tribune (city official) Marullus scolds the commoners for transferring their loyalties so quickly from the defeated and murdered general Pompey to the newly victorious Julius Caesar:

> Wherefore rejoice? What conquest brings he home?
> What tributaries follow him to Rome
> To grace in captive bonds his chariot wheels?
> You blocks, you stones, you worse than senseless
>   things!
> O you hard hearts, you cruel men of Rome,
> Knew you not Pompey? Many a time and oft
> Have you climbed up to walls and battlements,
> To towers and windows, yea, to chimney tops,
> Your infants in your arms, and there have sat
> The livelong day, with patient expectation,
> To see great Pompey pass the streets of Rome.

With the exception of one or two words like "wherefore" (which means "why," not "where"), "tributaries" (which means "captives"), and "patient expectation" (which means patient waiting), the meaning and emotions of this speech can be easily understood.

From here you can go on to dialogues or other more challenging scenes. Although you may stumble over unaccustomed phrases or unfamiliar words at first, and even fall flat when you're crossing some particularly rocky passages, pick yourself up and stay with it. Remember that it takes time to feel at home with anything new. Soon you'll come to recognize Shakespeare's unique sense of humor and way of saying things as easily as you recognize a friend's laughter.

And then it will just be a matter of choosing which one of Shakespeare's plays you want to tackle next. As a true fan of his, you'll find that you're constantly learning from his plays. It's a journey of discovery that you can continue for the rest of your life. For no matter how many times you read or see a particular play, there will always be something new there that you won't have noticed before.

Why do so many thousands of people get hooked on Shakespeare and develop a habit that lasts a lifetime? What can he really say to us today, in a world filled with inventions and problems he never could have imagined? And how do you get past his special language and difficult sentence structure to understand him?

The best way to answer these questions is to go see a live production. You might not know much about Shakespeare, or much about the theater, but when you watch actors performing one of his plays on the stage, it will soon become clear to you why people get so excited about a playwright who lived hundreds of years ago.

For the story—what's happening in the play—is the most accessible part of Shakespeare. In *A Midsummer Night's Dream*, for example, you can immediately understand the situation: a girl is chasing a guy who's chasing a girl who's chasing another guy. No wonder *A Midsummer Night's Dream* is one of the most popular of Shakespeare's plays: it's about one of the world's most popular pastimes— falling in love.

But the course of true love never did run smooth, as the young suitor Lysander says. Often in Shakespeare's comedies the girl whom the guy loves doesn't love him back, or she loves him but he loves someone else. In *The Two Gentlemen of Verona*, Julia loves Proteus, Proteus loves Sylvia, and Sylvia loves Valentine, who is Proteus's best friend. In the end, of course, true love prevails, but not without lots of complications along the way.

For in all of his plays—comedies, histories, and tragedies—Shakespeare is showing you human nature. His characters act and react in the most extraordinary ways—and sometimes in the most incomprehensible ways. People are always trying to find motivations for what a character does. They ask, "Why does Iago want to destroy Othello?"

The answer, to me, is very simple—because that's the way Iago is. That's just his nature. Shakespeare doesn't explain his characters; he sets them in motion—and away they go. He doesn't worry about whether they're likable or not. He's interested in interesting people, and his most fascinating characters are those who are unpredictable. If you lean back in your chair early on in one of his plays, thinking you've figured out what Iago or Shylock (in *The Merchant of Venice*) is up to, don't be too sure—because that great judge of human nature, Shakespeare, will surprise you every time.

He is just as wily in the way he structures a play. In *Macbeth*, a comic scene is suddenly introduced just after the bloodiest and most treacherous slaughter imaginable, of a guest and king by his host and subject, when in comes a drunk porter who has to go to the bathroom. Shakespeare is tickling your emotions by bringing a stand-up comic on-stage right on the heels of a savage murder.

It has taken me thirty years to understand even some of these things, and so I'm not suggesting that Shakespeare is immediately understandable. I've gotten to know him not through theory but through practice, the practice of the *living* Shakespeare—the playwright of the theater.

Of course the plays are a great achievement of dramatic literature, and they should be studied and analyzed in schools and universities. But you must always remember, when reading all the words *about* the playwright and his plays, that *Shakespeare's* words came first and that in the end there is nothing greater than a single actor on the stage speaking the lines of Shakespeare.

Everything important that I know about Shakespeare comes from the practical business of producing and directing his plays in the theater. The task of classifying, criticizing, and editing Shakespeare's printed works I happily leave to others. For me, his plays really do live on the stage, not on the page. That is what he wrote them for and that is how they are best appreciated.

Although Shakespeare lived and wrote hundreds of years ago, his name rolls off my tongue as if he were my brother. As a producer and director, I feel that there is a professional relationship between us that spans the centuries. As a human being, I feel that Shakespeare has enriched my understanding of life immeasurably. I hope you'll let him do the same for you.

❖

Much Ado about Nothing is a perennial delight onstage. In the first place, there's the wonderful relationship between Beatrice and Benedick, two people who are pretending they don't care for each other while they're actually falling in love. Once they're tricked into thinking that each loves the other, they suddenly change their minds and decide that it's destiny. Both of them reflect on this emotional about-face in wonderfully witty soliloquies. I especially like the way Benedick, the confirmed-bachelor-turned-lover, converts his logic to justify his newfound love for Beatrice: he says with a shrug, "the world must be peopled."

This movement from the resistance to the acceptance of love is a marvelous device in the play. It's just plain fun to watch and listen to Benedick and Beatrice, for "They never meet but there's a skirmish of wit between them." And yet I think Shakespeare is making a more profound point at the same time—that extreme emotion of one kind can also contain the opposite extreme: the initial dislike of Benedick for Beatrice and Beatrice for Benedick also holds within it the seeds of love.

The liveliness of this pair sometimes spills over into the other plot of the play, the more somber story of Hero and her fiance, Claudio, who rejects her at the altar because he thinks she's been unfaithful. It's not exactly a comic story, but into the midst of it skip Benedick and Beatrice with lines that, as I recall from the production I directed one summer, brought the house down every night. Beatrice has finally gotten Benedick to the point where he'll do anything to prove that he loves her: "Come, bid me do anything for thee," he begs her. Her two-word answer, straight to the point, is *"Kill Claudio."* The theater goes wild with laughter as the audience watches Benedick's ardor turn to dismay at the prospect of having to make good on a commitment to kill his best friend.

And finally, there is Dogberry, who can't use a word correctly to save his soul but is blissfully unaware of this disability. The way he pronounces grand-sounding words pompously—and incorrectly—is so funny that I can't help laughing out loud even when I'm sitting in a room by myself reading his speeches.

The scene where he is giving instructions to the officers

of the watch (3.3) is one of the funniest scenes ever written. He tells one fellow, "You are thought here to be the most *senseless* and fit man for the constable of the watch," and then addresses the group, "You shall also make no noise in the streets; for, for the watch to babble and to talk is most *tolerable* and not to be endured." Bidding them good night, he says "Adieu. Be *vigitant*, I beseech you." And in his last scene, instead of *begging* Leonato's permission to depart, he says, "I humbly *give you leave* to depart; and if a merry meeting may be wished, God *prohibit* it!"

Dogberry is such a delightful character, in a play full of delightful characters, that he never fails to amuse me. In fact, I could probably go on quoting his lines for the next ten pages, especially that wonderful scene with the watchmen. "First," he says, "who think you the most—" but perhaps I'll let you discover him for yourself.

JOSEPH PAPP

JOSEPH PAPP GRATEFULLY ACKNOWLEDGES THE HELP OF ELIZABETH KIRKLAND IN PREPARING THIS FOREWORD.

MUCH
ADO
ABOUT
NOTHING

Introduction

Much Ado about Nothing belongs to a group of Shakespeare's most mature romantic comedies, linked by similar titles, that also includes *As You Like It* and *Twelfth Night*. All date from the period 1598 to 1600. These plays are the culmination of Shakespeare's exuberant, philosophical, and festive vein in comedy, with only an occasional anticipation of the darker problem comedies of the early 1600s. They also parallel the culmination of Shakespeare's writing of history plays, in *Henry IV* and *V*.

Much Ado excels in combative wit and in swift, colloquial prose. It differs too from several other comedies (including *A Midsummer Night's Dream* and *The Merchant of Venice*) in that it features no journey of the lovers, no heroine disguised as a man, no envious court or city contrasted with an idealized landscape of the artist's imagination. Instead, the prevailing motif is that of the mask. Prominent scenes include a masked ball (2.1), a charade offstage in which the villainous Borachio misrepresents himself as the lover of Hero (actually Margaret in disguise), and a marriage ceremony with the supposedly dead bride masking as her own cousin (5.3). The word *Nothing* in the play's title, pronounced rather like *noting* in Elizabethan English, suggests a pun on the idea of overhearing as well as that of musical notation. Overhearings are constant and are essential to the process of both misunderstanding (as in the false rumor of Don Pedro's wooing Hero for himself) and clarification (as in the discovery by the night watch of the slander done to Hero's reputation, or in the revelation to Beatrice and Benedick of each other's true state of mind). The masks, or roles, that the characters incessantly assume are for the most part defensive and inimical to mutual understanding. How can they be dispelled? It is the search for candor and self-awareness in relationships with others, the quest for honesty and respect beneath conventional outward appearances, that provides the journey in this play.

Structurally the play contrasts two pairs of lovers. The young ladies, Beatrice and Hero, are cousins and close friends. The gentlemen, Benedick and Claudio, Italian gentlemen and fellow officers under the command of Don Pedro, have returned from the war in which they have fought bravely. These similarities chiefly serve, however, to accentuate the differences between the two couples. Hero is modest, retiring, usually silent, and obedient to her father's will. Claudio appears ideally suited to her, since he is also respectful and decorous. They are conventional lovers in the roles of romantic hero and ingenue heroine. Beatrice and Benedick, on the other hand, are renowned for "a kind of merry war" between them. Although obviously destined to come together, they are seemingly too independent and skeptical of convention to be tolerant and accepting in love. They scoff so at romantic sentimentality that they cannot permit themselves to drop their satirical masks. Yet paradoxically their relationship is the more surefooted because it is relentlessly probing and candid.

As in some of his other comic double plots (*The Taming of the Shrew*, for example), Shakespeare has linked together two stories of diverse origins and contrasting tones in order to set off one against the other. The Hero-Claudio plot is Italianate in flavor and origin, sensational, melodramatic, potentially tragic. In fact the often-told story of the maiden falsely slandered did frequently end in disaster—as, for example, in Edmund Spenser's *Faerie Queene*, 2.4 (1590). Spenser was apparently indebted to Ariosto's *Orlando Furioso* (translated into English by Sir John Harington, 1591), as were Peter Beverly in *The History of Ariodanto and Genevra* (1566) and Richard Mulcaster in his play *Ariodante and Genevora* (1583). Shakespeare seems to have relied more on the Italian version by Matteo Bandello (Lucca, 1554) and its French translation by Belleforest, *Histoires Tragiques* (1569). Still other versions have been discovered, both nondramatic and dramatic, although it cannot be established that Shakespeare was reworking an old play. Various factual inconsistencies in Shakespeare's text (such as Leonato's wife, Imogen, and a "kinsman" who are named briefly in both quarto and Folio but have no roles in the play) can perhaps be explained by Shakespeare's having worked quickly from more than one source.

Shakespeare's other plot, of Benedick and Beatrice, is much more English and his own. The battle of the sexes is a staple of English medieval humor (Chaucer's Wife of Bath, the Wakefield play of *Noah*) and of Shakespeare's own early comedy: Berowne and Rosaline in *Love's Labor's Lost*, Petruchio and Katharine in *The Taming of the Shrew*. The merry war of Benedick and Beatrice is Shakespeare's finest achievement in this vein, and was to become a rich legacy in the later English comedy of William Congreve, Oscar Wilde, and George Bernard Shaw. The tone is lighthearted, bantering, and reassuring, in contrast with the Italianate mood of vengeance and duplicity. No less English are the clownish antics of Dogberry and his crew, representing still another group of characters although not a separate plot. Like Constable Dull in *Love's Labor's Lost* or the tradesmen of *A Midsummer Night's Dream*, the buffoons of *Much Ado* function in a nominally Mediterranean setting, but are nonetheless recognizable London types. Their preposterous antics not only puncture the ominous mood threatening our enjoyment of the main plot but, absurdly enough, even help to abort a potential crime. When Dogberry comes, laughter cannot be far behind.

The two plots provide contrasting perspectives on the nature of love. Because it is sensational and melodramatic, the Claudio-Hero plot stresses situation at the expense of character. The conspiracy that nearly overwhelms the lovers is an engrossing story, but they themselves remain one-dimensional. They interest us more as conventional types, and hence as foils to Benedick and Beatrice, than as lovers in their own right. Benedick and Beatrice, on the other hand, are psychologically complex. Clearly they are fascinated with each other. Beatrice's questions in the first scene, although abusive in tone, betray her concern for Benedick's welfare. Has he safely returned from the wars? How did he bear himself in battle? Who are his companions? She tests his moral character by high standards, suspecting that he will fail because she demands so much. We are not surprised when she lectures her docile cousin, Hero, on the folly of submitting to parental choice in marriage: "It is my cousin's duty to make curtsy and say, 'Father, as it please you.' But yet for all that, cousin, let him be a handsome fellow, or else make another curtsy and say, 'Father, as it please me'" (2.1.49–52). Beatrice remains single not from love of spinsterhood but from insistence on a nearly perfect mate. Paradoxically, she who is the inveter-

ate scoffer is the true idealist. And we know from her un-
ceasing fascination with Benedick that he, of all the men in
her acquaintance, comes closest to her mark. The only fear
preventing the revelation of her love—a not unnatural fear,
in view of the insults she and Benedick exchange—is that he
will prove faithless and jest at her weakness.

Benedick is similarly hemmed in by his posturing as "a
professed tyrant to their sex" (1.1.161–162). Despite his reputation as a perennial bachelor, and his wry amusement at
Claudio's newfound passion, Benedick confesses in solilo-
quy (2.3.7–33) that he could be won to affection by the ideal
woman. Again his criteria are chiefly those of temperament
and moral character, although he by no means spurns
wealth, beauty, and social position; the happiest couples
are those well-matched in fortune's gifts. "Rich she shall
be, that's certain; wise, or I'll none; virtuous, or I'll never
cheapen her; fair, or I'll never look on her; mild, or come
not near me; noble, or not I for an angel; of good discourse,
an excellent musician, and her hair shall be of what color it
please God." This last self-mocking concession indicates
that Benedick is aware of how impossibly much he is asking. Still, there is one woman, Beatrice, who may well possess all of these qualities except mildness. Even her sharp
wit is part of her admirable intelligence. She is a match for
Benedick, and he is a man who would never tolerate the
submissive conventionality of someone like Hero. All that
appears to be lacking, in fact, is any sign of fondness on
Beatrice's part. For him to make overtures would be to in-
vite her withering scorn—not to mention the I-told-you-so
mockery of his friends.

Benedick and Beatrice have been playing the game of ver-
bal abuse for so long they scarcely remember how it
started—perhaps as a squaring-off between the only two in-
telligences worthy of contending with each other, perhaps
as a more profoundly defensive reaction of two sensitive
persons not willing to part lightly with their independence.
They seem to have had a prior relationship with each other
that ended unhappily. They know that true involvement
with others is a complex matter, one that can cause heartache. Yet the masks they wear with each other are scarcely
satisfactory. At the masked ball (2.1), we see how hurtful the
"merry war" has become. Benedick, attempting to pass

himself off as a stranger in a mask, abuses Beatrice by telling her of her reputation for disdain; but she, perceiving who he is, retaliates by telling him as a purported stranger what she "really" thinks of Benedick. These devices cut deeply, and confirm the worst fears of each. Ironically, these fears can be dispelled only by the virtuous deceptions practiced on them by their friends. Once Benedick is assured that Beatrice secretly loves him, masking her affection with scorn, he acquires the confidence he needs to make a commitment, and vice versa in her case. The beauty of the virtuous deceptions, moreover, is that they are so plausible—because, indeed, they are essentially true. Benedick overhears himself described as a person so satirical that Beatrice dare not reveal her affection, for fear of being repulsed (2.3). Beatrice learns that she is indeed called disdainful by her friends (3.1). Both lovers respond nobly to these revelations, accepting the accusations as richly deserved and placing no blame on the other. As Beatrice proclaims to herself, "Contempt, farewell, and maiden pride, adieu!" (l. 109). The relief afforded by this honesty is genuine and lasting.

Because Claudio knows so little about Hero, and is content with superficial expectations, he is vulnerable to a far more ugly sort of deception. Claudio's first questions about Hero betray his romantically stereotyped attitudes and his willingness to let Don Pedro and Hero's father, Leonato, arrange a financially advantageous match. Claudio treasures Hero's outward reputation for modesty, an appearance easily besmirched. When a false rumor suggests that Don Pedro is wooing the lady for himself, Claudio's response is predictably cliché-ridden: all's fair in love and war, you can't trust friends in an affair of the heart, and so farewell, Hero. The rumor has a superficial plausibility about it, especially when the villainous Don John steps into the situation. Motivated in part by pure malice and the sport of ruining others' happiness, John speaks to the masked Claudio at the ball (2.1) as though he were speaking to Benedick, and in this guise pretends to reveal the secret "fact" of Don Pedro's duplicity in love. (The device is precisely that used by Beatrice to put down Benedick in the same scene.) With this specious confirmation, Claudio leaps to a wrong conclusion, thereby judging both his friend and mistress to be false. He gives them no chance to speak in their own defense. To be sure, Hero's father and uncle have also believed in the false report and have welcomed the prospect of the wealthy Don Pedro as Hero's husband. The lady herself raises no objection to marriage with the older man. Still, Claudio has revealed a lack of faith resulting from his slender knowledge of Hero, and of himself.

The nearly tragic "demonstration" of Hero's infidelity follows the same course, because Claudio has not learned from his first experience. Once again the diabolical Don John first implants the insidious suggestion in Claudio's mind, then creates an illusion entirely plausible to the senses, and finally confirms it with Borachio's testimony. What Claudio and Don Pedro have actually seen is Margaret wooed at Hero's window, shrouded in the dark of night and seen from "afar off in the orchard." The power of suggestion is enough to do the rest. John's method, and his pleasure in evil, are much like those of his later counterparts, Iago in *Othello* and Edmund in *King Lear*. Indeed, John is compared with the devil, who has power over men's frail senses but must rely on their complicity and acquiescence in evil. Claudio is once again led to denounce faithlessly the virtuous woman whose loyalty he no longer deserves. Yet his fault is typically human, and is shared by Don Pedro. Providence gives him a second chance, through the ludicrous and bumbling intervention of Dogberry's night watch. These men overhear the plot of Don John as soon as it is announced to us, so that we know justice will eventually prevail even though it will also be farcically delayed. Once again, misunderstanding has become "much ado about nothing," an escalating of recriminations based on a purely chimerical assumption that must eventually be deflated. The painful experience is not without value, for it tests people's spiritual worth in a crisis. Beatrice, like Friar Francis, shows herself to be a person of unshakable faith in goodness. Benedick, though puzzled and torn in his loyalties, also passes the test and proves himself worthy of Beatrice. Claudio is found wanting, but Hero forgives and accepts him anyway. In her role as the granter of a merciful second chance, she foreshadows the beatifically symbolic nature of many of Shakespeare's later heroines.

Much Ado about Nothing comes closer perhaps to potentially tragic action than Shakespeare's other festive comedies. Virtually all the characters are affected by misunderstanding, resort to deception, or take refuge in protective masks. Candor and straightforwardness are ideals more easily praised than achieved. Even Benedick and Beatrice, marvelous though they may be, are far from perfect. Beatrice almost provokes Benedick into a vindictive and unnecessary murder. Despite their self-awareness, these lovers must be rescued from their isolation by a trick that ironically resembles the villainous practices of Don John. In this important sense, Benedick and Beatrice are not wholly unlike Claudio and Hero after all. Both pairs of lovers are saved from their own worst selves by a harmonizing force that works its will through strange and improbable means—even through Constable Dogberry and his watch.

Much Ado about Nothing
in Performance

Much Ado about Nothing has been popular onstage throughout virtually all of its history. According to the quarto of 1600 it was "sundry times publicly acted" by the Lord Chamberlain's men, and the play was performed at court in 1613 for the Princess Elizabeth and Frederick, Elector Palatine. Contemporary allusions in Shakespeare's day indicate that it was more highly regarded than Ben Jonson's writing in a similar vein, that is, in the social comedy of satirical wit. Leonard Digges, for example, while praising Jonson's sophisticated playwriting, admits Shakespeare's greater popularity: "let but Beatrice / And Benedick be seen; lo, in a trice, / The cockpit, galleries, boxes, all are full."

Restoration and eighteenth-century audiences, who tended to prefer comedy of manners to romance, felt comfortable with Shakespeare's play. *Much Ado* in fact became, more so than any other play Shakespeare wrote, a model for later English comedy: the agreeably sharp battle of the sexes between Benedick and Beatrice reemerges in William Congreve's *The Way of the World* (1700), Richard Sheridan's *The Rivals* (1775), Oscar Wilde's *The Importance of Being Earnest* (1895), George Bernard Shaw's *Man and Superman* (1905), and others.

Restoration and eighteenth-century dramatists did undertake to adapt the play, to be sure. William Davenant's *The Law Against Lovers*, at the theater in Lincoln's Inn Fields, London, in 1662, combined *Much Ado* with *Measure for Measure* by making Beatrice a ward of Lord Angelo and Benedick his brother. In this extraordinary situation, the two lovers are soon required to abandon their contest of wits and conspire instead to free Claudio (the Claudio of *Measure for Measure*) and his beloved Juliet, here Beatrice's cousin, from jail. Diarist Samuel Pepys saw the play and especially liked the dancing of the little girl, that is, Beatrice's younger sister Viola (from *Twelfth Night*), who sang a song written by Benedick and danced a saraband with castanets. In 1721 John Rich restored Shakespeare's text for a production at Lincoln's Inn Fields, but the newly restored text did not capture the stage. Charles Johnson's *Love in a Forest*, at the Theatre Royal, Drury Lane, in 1723, included parts of *Much Ado* (especially Benedick's role) in a version of *As You Like It*, and the Reverend James Miller's *The Universal Passion* (Drury Lane, 1737) combined *Much Ado* with Molière's *La Princesse d'Elide*.

Still, Shakespeare's own play (or something considerably closer to it), as interpreted by David Garrick and Hannah Pritchard, did become very popular at Drury Lane in 1748 and in subsequent years, so much so that Garrick chose the play for his great Shakespeare pageant at Drury Lane in 1769, following his Stratford-upon-Avon Jubilee. "Every scene between them," wrote a contemporary observer of Garrick and Pritchard, "was a continual struggle for superiority; nor could the spectators determine to which of them the preference was due." Garrick played Benedick for the last time in May of 1776 during his final year on the stage.

Actor-manager John Philip Kemble followed Garrick in a succession of memorable Benedicks. In April of 1788 at Drury Lane he played opposite Elizabeth Farren's Beatrice in a benefit performance for his wife Priscilla (who played Hero). Kemble continued to have great success with the play, which he regularly revived throughout his stay at Drury Lane. With his move to Covent Garden in 1803 his brother Charles became the principal actor playing Benedick, beginning with a production in John Philip Kemble's inaugural year of management. In 1836 Charles played the role opposite the nineteen-year-old Helen Faucit, in what was billed as his farewell performance on the stage. (In fact, he revived the role one more time, returning to the stage for four performances in 1840 at the request of Queen Victoria.) Faucit and then Ellen Terry starred as Beatrice, rescuing her from the shrewish interpretation common before that time; Faucit and Terry both favored a warmer, more animated, more buoyant mirth. Faucit played the role for a final time opposite Barry Sullivan at Stratford-upon-Avon in 1879 at the opening of the Shakespeare Memorial Theatre. Terry was paired with a deliberate and polished Henry Irving at the Lyceum Theatre in 1882 and subsequently at the Imperial Theatre in Westminster (1903) with Oscar Asche, in a production designed and directed by her son, Edward Gordon Craig. Beatrice was, along with Portia in *The Merchant of Venice*, the role for which Ellen Terry was best known and admired.

Nineteenth-century productions of *Much Ado* tended to be lavish. A contemporary account describes the stunning visual impression achieved by Charles Kean at the Princess's Theatre in 1838: "The opening view, the harbor of Messina, was quite a pictorial gem. The gradual illumination of the lighthouse and various mansions, in almost every window, the moon slowly rising and throwing silver light upon the deep blue waters of the Mediterranean, were managed with imposing reality. Then followed the masquerade, with its variegated lamps, bridge, gardens, and lake, seen through the arches of the palace." Henry Irving, in 1882, undertook to go even further. His scene opened on a classical structure of columns and yellow marble steps; the ballroom in Act 2 was done up in crimson and gold, with tapestries; the church scene had an ornamented canopied roof supported by massive pillars, iron gates, stained glass windows, a sumptuous altar, carved oak benches, hanging golden lamps, and statues of saints. Herbert Beerbohm Tree, at His Majesty's Theatre in 1905, provided Sicilian landscapes and Italian gardens to set off a dazzling orchestration of dances and masquerades.

Until the twentieth century, then, a common feature of production was the attempt to entertain through spectacle while focusing the comedy on the combat of wits between Benedick and Beatrice. Whether shrewish or good-natured in their badinage, these lovers were the center of the dramatic interest. More recent productions have tended to try something new by providing an entirely different setting for the action and by looking afresh at the lovers in the context of the whole play. Renaissance decor has not disappeared, of course, as in the influential production directed by John Gielgud at Stratford-upon-Avon in 1949, later with Gielgud himself and Peggy Ashcroft in the chief roles during a revival in 1950. Other directors, however, have chosen for their locations the American Southwest of fast guns and frontier justice with Dogberry as a bumbling sheriff (directed by John Houseman and Jack Landau at Stratford, Connecticut, in 1957), the early Victorian era of

crinolines, parasols, and tight lacing (directed by Douglas
Seale, Stratford-upon-Avon in 1958), the Regency England
of Wellington uniforms (Michael Langham, Stratford-upon-
Avon, 1961), the turn-of-the-century Sicily of broiling sun
and hot temperament (Franco Zeffirelli, National Theatre,
1965), the Edwardian England of bicycle-riding New
Women (William Hutt, Stratford, Canada, 1971), and the
small-town America of the post-Spanish-American War era
of Teddy Roosevelt, gramophones, brass bands, high wing
collars, and Keystone cops (A. J. Antoon, Delacorte Theater,
New York, 1972). (Antoon's production, when it was shown
subsequently on commercial television, landed at the bot-
tom of the weekly Nielsen ratings and yet was seen on that
occasion by more people than in all the play's previous theatrical history.) In 1976 at Stratford-upon-Avon, John Barton set the play in the Victorian India of the British Raj.
Six years later Terry Hands, again at Stratford, returned
the play close to its original setting by locating it in Caroline England.

By relocating the play, twentieth-century directors have
uncovered darker and more complex issues than those generally confronted by eighteenth- and nineteenth-century
productions. Zeffirelli sought to illuminate Hero's plight in
the milieu of the Sicilian code of machismo and its fierce
demands for female chastity. The British Raj in India provided Barton a world of class-conscious privilege and
imperialist mentality in the context of which Claudio's self-
centered caddishness and Don John's wanton cruelty
seemed plausible and even predictable. Small-town America gave Antoon a more genial, if parochial, perspective on
the lovers' tribulations, and the Keystone cops, with their
frantic slapstick chases in the idiom of silent film, were ultimately as ineffectual as the melodramatic Don John,
whom they almost unintentionally managed to bring to
ground. Regency England established a mood of carefree
affluence that gave credibility to the plots and machina-
tions of bored aristocrats. Hands's Caroline setting provided a world of aristocratic privilege where feeling was
easily sacrificed to fashion; the superficial values of Messinan society were literally reflected in the mirrored floor
and Plexiglas panels of Ralph Koltai's set. Occasionally
these productions strained their audiences' credulity by

making nonsense of the play's ceremonial language—what is one to make of "Your Grace" and "my lord" in frontier Texas?—and thus prompted arguments about the virtues and defects of "relevance" in the theater. But at their best such recent productions have done much to explore what is genuinely timeless in *Much Ado* and to discover the balance among its various parts, which earlier productions generally had ignored in favor of the star system of casting.

Staging requirements in the text itself call not only for balance but for juxtaposition. Overheard conversations are frequent, inviting the director to see a resemblance between innocent and vicious modes of deception. Because there is so much playacting and deception, the play calls attention to its own devices of illusion. (This must have been especially true on the Elizabethan stage where, in the absence of scenery, the actors suggested concealment by hiding behind onstage pillars and the like; possibly Beatrice hid herself in her "pleachèd bower" in Act 3, scene 1, by means of a curtained wall, or discovery space, that is, a recessed area, at the rear of the stage.) Characters in the play are incessantly stage-managing scenes of mistaken impressions: Benedick's friends devise a conversation for him to overhear, and Beatrice's friends do the same for her, while Don John improvises a trap for Claudio at the masked ball and then stages a scene of infidelity at Beatrice's window. Masking is not only a device of plot; in the theater it is also a visual metaphor of the roles that characters adopt toward one another. The masked ball is more than a merry occasion; it becomes a pattern for the dancing partners that expresses through their movements the intricate and dangerous rituals of courtship. Dogberry and his watch are funny in part because they are so apart from this courtly world of dance and wit combat, inferior in intelligence and social grace and yet, paradoxically, able to offer the kind of humorous corrective that simplicity and artlessness alone can provide.

The Playhouse

This early copy of a drawing by Johannes de Witt of the Swan Theatre in London (c. 1596), made by his friend Arend van Buchell, is the only surviving contemporary sketch of the interior of a public theater in the 1590s.

From other contemporary evidence, including the stage directions and dialogue of Elizabethan plays, we can surmise that the various public theaters where Shakespeare's plays were produced (the Theatre, the Curtain, the Globe) resembled the Swan in many important particulars, though there must have been some variations as well. The public playhouses were essentially round, or polygonal, and open to the sky, forming an acting arena approximately 70 feet in diameter; they did not have a large curtain with which to open and close a scene, such as we see today in opera and some traditional theater. A platform measuring approximately 43 feet across and 27 feet deep, referred to in the de Witt drawing as the *proscaenium*, projected into the yard, *planities sive arena*. The roof, *tectum*, above the stage and supported by two pillars, could contain machinery for ascents and descents, as were required in several of Shakespeare's late plays. Above this roof was a hut, shown in the drawing with a flag flying atop it and a trumpeter at its door announcing the performance of a play. The underside of the stage roof, called the heavens, was usually richly decorated with symbolic figures of the sun, the moon, and the constellations. The platform stage stood at a height of 5$\frac{1}{2}$ feet or so above the yard, providing room under the stage for underworldly effects. A trapdoor, which is not visible in this drawing, gave access to the space below.

The structure at the back of the platform (labeled *mimorum aedes*), known as the tiring-house because it was the actors' attiring (dressing) space, featured at least two doors, as shown here. Some theaters seem to have also had a discovery space, or curtained recessed alcove, perhaps between the two doors—in which Falstaff could have hidden from the sheriff (*1 Henry IV*, 2.4) or Polonius could have eavesdropped on Hamlet and his mother (*Hamlet*, 3.4). This discovery space probably gave the actors a means of access to and from the tiring-house. Curtains may also have been hung in front of the stage doors on occasion. The de Witt drawing shows a gallery above the doors that extends across the back and evidently contains spectators. On occasions when action "above" demanded the use of this space, as when Juliet appears at her "window" (*Romeo and Juliet*, 2.2 and 3.5), the gallery seems to have been used by the actors, but large scenes there were impractical.

The three-tiered auditorium is perhaps best described by Thomas Platter, a visitor to London in 1599 who saw on that occasion Shakespeare's *Julius Caesar* performed at the Globe:

The playhouses are so constructed that they play on a raised platform, so that everyone has a good view. There are different galleries and places [*orchestra, sedilia, porticus*], however, where the seating is better and more comfortable and therefore more expensive. For whoever cares to stand below only pays one English penny, but if he wishes to sit, he enters by another door [*ingressus*] and pays another penny, while if he desires to sit in the most comfortable seats, which are cushioned, where he not only sees everything well but can also be seen, then he pays yet another English penny at another door. And during the performance food and drink are carried round the audience, so that for what one cares to pay one may also have refreshment.

Scenery was not used, though the theater building itself was handsome enough to invoke a feeling of order and hierarchy that lent itself to the splendor and pageantry onstage. Portable properties, such as thrones, stools, tables, and beds, could be carried or thrust on as needed. In the scene pictured here by de Witt, a lady on a bench, attended perhaps by her waiting-gentlewoman, receives the address of a male figure. If Shakespeare had written *Twelfth Night* by 1596 for performance at the Swan, we could imagine Malvolio appearing like this as he bows before the Countess Olivia and her gentlewoman, Maria.

MUCH
ADO
ABOUT
NOTHING

[*Dramatis Personae*

DON PEDRO, *Prince of Aragon*
LEONATO, *Governor of Messina*
ANTONIO, *his brother*

BENEDICK, *a young lord of Padua*
BEATRICE, *Leonato's niece*
CLAUDIO, *a young lord of Florence*
HERO, *Leonato's daughter*
MARGARET,
URSULA, } *gentlewomen attending Hero*

DON JOHN, *Don Pedro's bastard brother*
BORACHIO,
CONRADE, } *followers of Don John*

DOGBERRY, *Constable in charge of the Watch*
VERGES, *the Headborough, or parish constable, Dogberry's partner*
A SEXTON
FIRST WATCHMAN
SECOND WATCHMAN (GEORGE SEACOAL)

BALTHASAR, *a singer attending Don Pedro*
FRIAR FRANCIS
A BOY
MESSENGER *to Leonato*
Another MESSENGER

Attendants, Musicians, Members of the Watch, Antonio's Son and other Kinsmen

SCENE: *Messina*]

1.1 *Enter Leonato, Governor of Messina, Hero his
daughter, and Beatrice his niece, with a
Messenger.*

LEONATO [*Holding a letter*]   I learn in this letter that Don
  Pedro of Aragon comes this night to Messina.
MESSENGER   He is very near by this. He was not three
  leagues off when I left him.
LEONATO   How many gentlemen have you lost in this
  action?   6
MESSENGER   But few of any sort and none of name.   7
LEONATO   A victory is twice itself when the achiever
  brings home full numbers. I find here that Don Pedro
  hath bestowed much honor on a young Florentine
  called Claudio.
MESSENGER   Much deserved on his part and equally re-   12
  membered by Don Pedro. He hath borne himself be-   13
  yond the promise of his age, doing, in the figure of a
  lamb, the feats of a lion. He hath indeed better bettered   15
  expectation than you must expect of me to tell you
  how.
LEONATO   He hath an uncle here in Messina will be very   18
  much glad of it.
MESSENGER   I have already delivered him letters, and
  there appears much joy in him, even so much that joy
  could not show itself modest enough without a badge   22
  of bitterness.   23
LEONATO   Did he break out into tears?
MESSENGER   In great measure.
LEONATO   A kind overflow of kindness. There are no   26
  faces truer than those that are so washed. How much
  better is it to weep at joy than to joy at weeping!
BEATRICE   I pray you, is Signor Mountanto returned   29
  from the wars or no?
MESSENGER   I know none of that name, lady. There was
  none such in the army of any sort.

1.1. Location: Messina. Before Leonato's house.
6 action battle   **7 sort** rank.   **name** reputation, or noble name
12–13 remembered rewarded   **15 bettered** surpassed   **18 will** who
will   **22 modest** moderate   **22–23 badge of bitterness** sign of sorrow,
i.e., tears   **26 kind** natural   **29 Mountanto** montanto, an upward blow
or thrust in fencing

LEONATO   What is he that you ask for, niece?

HERO   My cousin means Signor Benedick of Padua.

MESSENGER   O, he's returned, and as pleasant as ever he 35
was.

BEATRICE   He set up his bills here in Messina and chal- 37
lenged Cupid at the flight; and my uncle's fool, reading 38
the challenge, subscribed for Cupid and challenged 39
him at the bird-bolt. I pray you, how many hath he 40
killed and eaten in these wars? But how many hath he
killed? For indeed I promised to eat all of his killing.

LEONATO   Faith, niece, you tax Signor Benedick too 43
much, but he'll be meet with you, I doubt it not. 44

MESSENGER   He hath done good service, lady, in these
wars.

BEATRICE   You had musty victual, and he hath holp to 47
eat it. He is a very valiant trencherman; he hath an 48
excellent stomach. 49

MESSENGER   And a good soldier too, lady.

BEATRICE   And a good soldier to a lady, but what is he
to a lord? 52

MESSENGER   A lord to a lord, a man to a man, stuffed
with all honorable virtues.

BEATRICE   It is so indeed; he is no less than a stuffed 55
man. But for the stuffing—well, we are all mortal. 56

LEONATO   You must not, sir, mistake my niece. There is
a kind of merry war betwixt Signor Benedick and her.
They never meet but there's a skirmish of wit between
them.

BEATRICE   Alas! He gets nothing by that. In our last con-
flict, four of his five wits went halting off, and now is 62

---

35 pleasant jocular   **37 bills** placards, advertisements   **37–38 challenged . . . flight** undertook to rival Cupid as an archer   **38 my uncle's
fool** (Perhaps a professional fool in her uncle's service; possibly Beatrice means herself, recalling an earlier flirtation with Benedick.)
39 subscribed for accepted on behalf of   **40 bird-bolt** a blunt-headed
arrow used for fowling (sometimes used by children because of its
relative harmlessness and thus conventionally appropriate to Cupid)
43 tax disparage   **44 meet** even, quits   **47 musty victual** stale food).
holp helped   **48 valiant trencherman** great eater   **49 stomach** appetite   **52 to** compared to   **55–56 stuffed man** i.e., a figure stuffed to
resemble a man   **56 the stuffing** i.e., what he's truly made of.   **well . . .
mortal** i.e., well, we all have our faults   **62 five wits** i.e., not the five
senses, but the five faculties: memory, imagination, judgment, fantasy,
common wit.   **halting** limping

the whole man governed with one; so that if he have
wit enough to keep himself warm, let him bear it for
a difference between himself and his horse, for it is all 65
the wealth that he hath left to be known a reasonable 66
creature. Who is his companion now? He hath every
month a new sworn brother. 68

MESSENGER   Is 't possible?

BEATRICE   Very easily possible. He wears his faith but 70
as the fashion of his hat; it ever changes with the next
block. 72

MESSENGER   I see, lady, the gentleman is not in your 73
books. 74

BEATRICE   No; an he were, I would burn my study. But 75
I pray you, who is his companion? Is there no young
squarer now that will make a voyage with him to the 77
devil?

MESSENGER   He is most in the company of the right noble Claudio.

BEATRICE   O Lord, he will hang upon him like a disease! 81
He is sooner caught than the pestilence, and the taker
runs presently mad. God help the noble Claudio! If he 83
have caught the Benedick, it will cost him a thousand 84
pound ere 'a be cured. 85

MESSENGER   I will hold friends with you, lady. 86

BEATRICE   Do, good friend.

LEONATO   You will never run mad, niece. 88

BEATRICE   No, not till a hot January.

MESSENGER   Don Pedro is approached.

*Enter Don Pedro, Claudio, Benedick, Balthasar,
and [Don] John the Bastard.*

DON PEDRO   Good Signor Leonato, are you come to

---

65 difference heraldic distinguishing feature (with a play on the usual
sense). **is** i.e., takes   **66 to be known** i.e., in order that he may be
recognized as   **68 sworn brother** brother in arms. (*Frater juratus,* an
allusion to the ancient practice of swearing brotherhood.)   **70 faith**
allegiance, or fidelity   **72 block** mold for shaping hats   **73–74 in your
books** i.e., in favor with you, in your account books for credit   **75 an** if
(also in l. 131)   **77 squarer** quarreler   **81 he** i.e., Benedick   **83 presently**
immediately   **84 the Benedick** i.e., as if he were a disease   **85 'a** he
86 hold friends keep on friendly terms (so as not to earn your enmity)
88 run mad i.e., "catch the Benedick"

meet your trouble? The fashion of the world is to avoid 92
cost, and you encounter it. 93

LEONATO Never came trouble to my house in the likeness of Your Grace. For trouble being gone, comfort
should remain; but when you depart from me, sorrow
abides and happiness takes his leave.

DON PEDRO You embrace your charge too willingly.—I 98
think this is your daughter.

                  [*Presenting himself to Hero.*]

LEONATO Her mother hath many times told me so.

BENEDICK Were you in doubt, sir, that you asked her?

LEONATO Signor Benedick, no; for then were you a
child.

DON PEDRO You have it full, Benedick. We may guess 104
by this what you are, being a man. Truly, the lady
fathers herself. Be happy, lady, for you are like an hon- 106
orable father.

BENEDICK If Signor Leonato be her father, she would
not have his head on her shoulders for all Messina, as 109
like him as she is.

              [*Don Pedro and Leonato talk aside.*]

BEATRICE I wonder that you will still be talking, Signor
Benedick. Nobody marks you.

BENEDICK What, my dear Lady Disdain! Are you yet
living?

BEATRICE Is it possible disdain should die while she
hath such meet food to feed it as Signor Benedick? 116
Courtesy itself must convert to disdain, if you come in 117
her presence.

BENEDICK Then is courtesy a turncoat. But it is certain
I am loved of all ladies, only you excepted; and I would
I could find in my heart that I had not a hard heart, for
truly I love none.

BEATRICE A dear happiness to women! They would 123
else have been troubled with a pernicious suitor. I

---

92 your trouble i.e., the expense of entertaining me and my retinue
93 encounter go to meet **98 embrace your charge** greet your burden
104 have it full are well answered **106 fathers herself** shows by appearance who her father is **109 his head** i.e., with Leonato's white beard
and signs of age **116 meet** suitable (with a pun on *meat*) **117 convert**
change **123 dear happiness** precious good luck

thank God and my cold blood I am of your humor for 125
that. I had rather hear my dog bark at a crow than a 126
man swear he loves me.

BENEDICK   God keep your ladyship still in that mind! So
some gentleman or other shall scape a predestinate 129
scratched face.

BEATRICE   Scratching could not make it worse, an 'twere
such a face as yours were.   132

BENEDICK   Well, you are a rare parrot-teacher.   133

BEATRICE   A bird of my tongue is better than a beast of 134
yours.   135

BENEDICK   I would my horse had the speed of your
tongue and so good a continuer. But keep your way, 137
i' God's name; I have done.

BEATRICE   You always end with a jade's trick. I know 139
you of old.

DON PEDRO   That is the sum of all, Leonato. Signor 141
Claudio and Signor Benedick, my dear friend Leonato
hath invited you all. I tell him we shall stay here at the
least a month, and he heartily prays some occasion
may detain us longer. I dare swear he is no hypocrite
but prays from his heart.

LEONATO   If you swear, my lord, you shall not be for-
sworn. [*To Don John.*] Let me bid you welcome, my
lord, being reconciled to the Prince your brother. I owe 149
you all duty.

DON JOHN   I thank you. I am not of many words, but I
thank you.

LEONATO   Please it Your Grace lead on?

DON PEDRO   Your hand, Leonato. We will go together.   154
                    Exeunt. Manent Benedick and Claudio.

125–126 I am . . . that I am of the same disposition in that matter, i.e., of
loving no one   **129 scape** escape.   **predestinate** inevitable (for any man
who should woo Beatrice)   **132 were** i.e., is   **133 rare** outstanding.
parrot-teacher i.e., one who would teach a parrot well, because you say
the same things over and over   **134 of my tongue** taught to speak like me,
i.e., incessantly   **134–135 of yours** taught to speak like you   **137 a continuer** i.e., in staying power   **139 a jade's trick** i.e., an ill-tempered horse's
habit of slipping its head out of the collar (as Benedick does in this race
of wits)   **141 sum of all** (Don Pedro and Leonato have been conversing
apart on other matters.)   **149 being** since you are   **154 go together** i.e.,
arm in arm (thus avoiding the question of precedence in order of leaving)

CLAUDIO Benedick, didst thou note the daughter of Signor Leonato?

BENEDICK I noted her not, but I looked on her. 157

CLAUDIO Is she not a modest young lady?

BENEDICK Do you question me as an honest man should do, for my simple true judgment? Or would you have me speak after my custom, as being a professed tyrant to their sex? 162

CLAUDIO No, I pray thee, speak in sober judgment.

BENEDICK Why, i' faith, methinks she's too low for a 164 high praise, too brown for a fair praise, and too little for a great praise. Only this commendation I can afford her, that were she other than she is, she were unhandsome, and being no other but as she is, I do not like her.

CLAUDIO Thou thinkest I am in sport. I pray thee, tell me truly how thou lik'st her.

BENEDICK Would you buy her, that you inquire after her?

CLAUDIO Can the world buy such a jewel?

BENEDICK Yea, and a case to put it into. But speak you 175 this with a sad brow? Or do you play the flouting Jack, 176 to tell us Cupid is a good hare-finder and Vulcan a rare 177 carpenter? Come, in what key shall a man take you, to 178 go in the song? 179

CLAUDIO In mine eye she is the sweetest lady that ever I looked on.

BENEDICK I can see yet without spectacles, and I see no such matter. There's her cousin, an she were not possessed with a fury, exceeds her as much in beauty as the first of May doth the last of December. But I hope you have no intent to turn husband, have you?

CLAUDIO I would scarce trust myself, though I had sworn the contrary, if Hero would be my wife.

BENEDICK Is 't come to this? In faith, hath not the world

---

157 noted her not gave her no special attention **162 tyrant** one cruel or pitiless in attitude **164 low** short **175 case** (1) jewel case (2) clothing, outer garments. (There is also a bawdy play on the meaning "female pudenda.") **176 sad** serious. **flouting Jack** i.e., mocking rascal **177–178 to tell . . . carpenter** i.e., are you mocking us with nonsense? (Cupid was blind, not sharp-eyed like a hunter, and Vulcan was a blacksmith, not a carpenter.) **179 go in** join in, harmonize with

one man but he will wear his cap with suspicion? Shall 190
I never see a bachelor of threescore again? Go to,
i' faith; an thou wilt needs thrust thy neck into a yoke,
wear the print of it and sigh away Sundays. Look, Don 193
Pedro is returned to seek you.

Enter Don Pedro.

DON PEDRO   What secret hath held you here, that you
followed not to Leonato's?

BENEDICK   I would Your Grace would constrain me to 197
tell.

DON PEDRO   I charge thee on thy allegiance.

BENEDICK   You hear, Count Claudio. I can be secret as
a dumb man—I would have you think so—but on
my allegiance, mark you this, on my allegiance! He is
in love. With who? Now that is Your Grace's part. 203
Mark how short his answer is: with Hero, Leonato's
short daughter.

CLAUDIO   If this were so, so were it uttered.   206

BENEDICK   Like the old tale, my lord: "It is not so, nor 207
'twas not so, but indeed, God forbid it should be so."

CLAUDIO   If my passion change not shortly, God forbid
it should be otherwise.

DON PEDRO   Amen, if you love her, for the lady is very
well worthy.

CLAUDIO   You speak this to fetch me in, my lord.   213

DON PEDRO   By my troth, I speak my thought.

CLAUDIO   And in faith, my lord, I spoke mine.

BENEDICK   And by my two faiths and troths, my lord,
I spoke mine.

---

190 wear . . . suspicion i.e., marry and thus be suspected of wearing his
cap to hide his cuckold's horns, signs of his wife's infidelity   **193 print**
imprint.   **Sundays** i.e., when, owing to the domesticity of the day, you
cannot escape from your yokefellow   **197 constrain** order   **203 part**
speaking part (i.e., to say, "With who?")   **206 If this . . . uttered** i.e., if I
really were in love with Hero and told Benedick, he would blab the
secret this way   **207 old tale** (In the English fairy tale known as "Mr.
Fox," a murderous wooer, discovered in his crimes by the lady he seeks
to marry and victimize, repeatedly disclaims her recital of what she has
seen by the refrain here set in quotations. The story is a variant of the
theme known as "the Robber Bridegroom." Benedick uses it mockingly
here to characterize Claudio's reluctance to admit his "crime" of falling
in love.)   **213 fetch me in** get me to confess

CLAUDIO   That I love her, I feel.

DON PEDRO   That she is worthy, I know.

BENEDICK   That I neither feel how she should be loved nor know how she should be worthy is the opinion that fire cannot melt out of me. I will die in it at the stake.

DON PEDRO   Thou wast ever an obstinate heretic in the despite of beauty.   225

CLAUDIO   And never could maintain his part but in the force of his will.   227

BENEDICK   That a woman conceived me, I thank her; that she brought me up, I likewise give her most humble thanks. But that I will have a recheat winded in my   230
forehead or hang my bugle in an invisible baldrick,   231
all women shall pardon me. Because I will not do them the wrong to mistrust any, I will do myself the right to trust none; and the fine is, for the which I may go the   234
finer, I will live a bachelor.   235

DON PEDRO   I shall see thee, ere I die, look pale with love.

BENEDICK   With anger, with sickness, or with hunger, my lord, not with love. Prove that ever I lose more   239
blood with love than I will get again with drinking,   240
pick out mine eyes with a ballad-maker's pen and   241
hang me up at the door of a brothel house for the sign   242
of blind Cupid.

DON PEDRO   Well, if ever thou dost fall from this faith, thou wilt prove a notable argument.   245

BENEDICK   If I do, hang me in a bottle like a cat and   246

225 despite contempt   **227 force of his will** i.e., refusing to be guided by reason (which, as defined by the Schoolmen, was the state of the heretic)   **230–232 But that . . . me** i.e., women must pardon me for refusing to have my horn placed on my head (like a cuckold)   **230 recheat** hunting call sounded (*winded*) on a horn to assemble the hounds   **231 baldrick** strap that supports the horn (here invisible because the horn is the metaphorical one of cuckoldry)   **234 fine** end   **234–235 go the finer** be more finely dressed (since without a wife I will have more money to spend on clothing)   **239 Prove** if you can prove   **239–240 lose . . . drinking** (According to Elizabethan theory, each sigh cost the heart a drop of blood, whereas blood was replenished by wine.)   **241 ballad-maker's pen** i.e., such as would be used to write love ballads or satires   **242 sign** a painted sign, such as hung over inns and shops   **245 notable argument** notorious subject for conversation, example   **246 bottle** wicker or leather basket (to hold the cat sometimes used as an archery target)

shoot at me, and he that hits me, let him be clapped on
the shoulder and called Adam.   248

DON PEDRO Well, as time shall try:
"In time the savage bull doth bear the yoke."   250

BENEDICK The savage bull may; but if ever the sensible
Benedick bear it, pluck off the bull's horns and set
them in my forehead, and let me be vilely painted,
and in such great letters as they write, "Here is good
horse to hire," let them signify under my sign, "Here
you may see Benedick the married man."

CLAUDIO If this should ever happen, thou wouldst be
horn-mad.   258

DON PEDRO Nay, if Cupid have not spent all his quiver
in Venice, thou wilt quake for this shortly.   260

BENEDICK I look for an earthquake too, then.   261

DON PEDRO Well, you will temporize with the hours. In   262
the meantime, good Signor Benedick, repair to Leonato's. Commend me to him, and tell him I will not fail
him at supper, for indeed he hath made great preparation.

BENEDICK I have almost matter enough in me for such   267
an embassage; and so I commit you—   268

CLAUDIO To the tuition of God. From my house, if I had   269
it—

DON PEDRO The sixth of July. Your loving friend, Benedick.

BENEDICK Nay, mock not, mock not. The body of your
discourse is sometimes guarded with fragments, and   274
the guards are but slightly basted on neither. Ere you 275

---

248 Adam (Probably refers to Adam Bell, archer outlaw of the ballads.) **250 In . . . yoke** (Proverbial; also appearing in a varied form in
Kyd's *The Spanish Tragedy*, 2.1.) **258 horn-mad** stark mad. (From the
fury of horned beasts; with allusion to cuckoldry.) **260 Venice** (A city
noted for licentiousness.) **quake** (with a pun on *quiver* in the previous
line) **261 I . . . then** i.e., my falling in love will be at least as rare as an
earthquake **262 temporize . . . hours** come to terms, or become milder,
in time (with perhaps a bawdy pun on *hours, whores;* pronounced
something like "hoors") **267 matter** wit, intelligence **268 embassage**
mission. **and so . . . you** (A conventional close, which Claudio and Don
Pedro mockingly play with as though it were the complimentary close
of a letter.) **269 tuition** protection **274 guarded** ornamented,
trimmed **275 guards . . . neither** trimmings are tenuously stitched on
at best, have only the flimsiest connection

flout old ends any further, examine your conscience. 276
And so I leave you.   *Exit.*

CLAUDIO
My liege, Your Highness now may do me good.   278

DON PEDRO
My love is thine to teach. Teach it but how,
And thou shalt see how apt it is to learn
Any hard lesson that may do thee good.

CLAUDIO
Hath Leonato any son, my lord?

DON PEDRO
No child but Hero; she's his only heir.
Dost thou affect her, Claudio?

CLAUDIO   O my lord,   284
When you went onward on this ended action,   285
I looked upon her with a soldier's eye,
That liked, but had a rougher task in hand
Than to drive liking to the name of love.
But now I am returned and that war thoughts   289
Have left their places vacant, in their rooms
Come thronging soft and delicate desires,
All prompting me how fair young Hero is,
Saying I liked her ere I went to wars.

DON PEDRO
Thou wilt be like a lover presently
And tire the hearer with a book of words.
If thou dost love fair Hero, cherish it,
And I will break with her and with her father,   297
And thou shalt have her. Was 't not to this end
That thou began'st to twist so fine a story?   299

CLAUDIO
How sweetly you do minister to love,
That know love's grief by his complexion!   301
But lest my liking might too sudden seem,
I would have salved it with a longer treatise.   303

276 flout old ends quote or recite mockingly proverbial tags of wisdom
(as well as the *ends* of letters that Claudio and Don Pedro have been
parodying).   **examine your conscience** look to your own behavior or
speech   **278 do me good** do me some good, help me   **284 affect** love
285 ended action military action now ended   **289 now** now that
297 break open the subject (as also in l. 314)   **299 twist** draw out the
thread of   **301 his complexion** its outward appearance   **303 salved** i.e.,
accounted for, explained

DON PEDRO
What need the bridge much broader than the flood?   304
The fairest grant is the necessity.   305
Look what will serve is fit. 'Tis once, thou lovest,   306
And I will fit thee with the remedy.
I know we shall have reveling tonight;
I will assume thy part in some disguise
And tell fair Hero I am Claudio,
And in her bosom I'll unclasp my heart
And take her hearing prisoner with the force   312
And strong encounter of my amorous tale.
Then after to her father will I break,
And the conclusion is, she shall be thine.
In practice let us put it presently.   *Exeunt.*

❖

1.2   *Enter Leonato and an old man [Antonio],*
     brother to Leonato, [meeting].

LEONATO   How now, brother! Where is my cousin,   1
   your son? Hath he provided this music?
ANTONIO   He is very busy about it. But brother, I can
   tell you strange news that you yet dreamt not of.
LEONATO   Are they good?   5
ANTONIO   As the event stamps them, but they have a   6
   good cover; they show well outward. The Prince and   7
   Count Claudio, walking in a thick-pleached alley in   8
   mine orchard, were thus much overheard by a man of   9
   mine: the Prince discovered to Claudio that he loved   10
   my niece your daughter and meant to acknowledge it

304 What need why need be.   **flood** river   **305 The . . . necessity** the
best gift is one that is really needed   **306 Look what** whatever.   **'Tis
once** in short, the fact is. (This speech of Don Pedro's is overheard by a
servant of Antonio's, as we learn in the next scene.)   **312 take . . .
prisoner** i.e., command her attention and assent

1.2. Location: Leonato's house.
1 cousin kinsman   **5 they** i.e., the news (often treated as a plural noun,
as at 2.1.167)   **6 event** outcome   **6–7 stamps . . . cover** (The image is of
news that is printed and bound in a book; Antonio means that things
look promising at the moment and will be good indeed if they turn out
so.)   **8 thick-pleached alley** walk lined with dense hedges of intertwined
shrubs   **9 orchard** garden   **10 discovered** disclosed

this night in a dance, and if he found her accordant, 12
he meant to take the present time by the top and in- 13
stantly break with you of it.

LEONATO   Hath the fellow any wit that told you this?   15

ANTONIO   A good sharp fellow. I will send for him, and
question him yourself.

LEONATO   No, no; we will hold it as a dream till it ap- 18
pear itself. But I will acquaint my daughter withal, that 19
she may be the better prepared for an answer, if per- 20
adventure this be true. Go you and tell her of it. [*Enter* 21
Antonio's Son, with a Musician, and Others.] Cousins,
you know what you have to do.—O, I cry you mercy, 23
friend; go you with me, and I will use your skill.— 24
Good cousin, have a care this busy time.   *Exeunt.* 25

✣

1.3   *Enter Sir [Don] John the Bastard and Conrade,*
his companion.

CONRADE   What the goodyear, my lord! Why are you 1
thus out of measure sad?   2

DON JOHN   There is no measure in the occasion that
breeds; therefore the sadness is without limit.   4

CONRADE   You should hear reason.   5

DON JOHN   And when I have heard it, what blessing
brings it?

CONRADE   If not a present remedy, at least a patient suf- 8
ferance.   9

DON JOHN   I wonder that thou, being, as thou sayst

---

12 **accordant** agreeing, consenting   13 **take . . . top** i.e., seize the opportunity. (Proverbially, Time was imagined bald in the back of the head
but with a forelock of hair in the front that opportunistically could be
grabbed.)   15 **wit** sense, intelligence   18–19 **till . . . itself** till it mani-
fests itself   20–21 **peradventure** by chance   23 **cry you mercy** beg your
pardon   24 **friend** (Addressed perhaps to the musician.)   25 **have . . .**
time i.e., take care of yourself

1.3. Location: Leonato's house.
1 **What the goodyear** (An unexplained expletive, perhaps suggesting
disgust, like "What the deuce.")   2 **out of measure** immoderately
4 **breeds** causes (it)   5 **hear** listen to   8–9 **sufferance** endurance

thou art, born under Saturn, goest about to apply a 11
moral medicine to a mortifying mischief. I cannot hide 12
what I am: I must be sad when I have cause and smile
at no man's jests, eat when I have stomach and wait 14
for no man's leisure, sleep when I am drowsy and tend 15
on no man's business, laugh when I am merry and 16
claw no man in his humor.   17

CONRADE   Yea, but you must not make the full show of
this till you may do it without controlment. You have 19
of late stood out against your brother, and he hath 20
ta'en you newly into his grace, where it is impossible 21
you should take true root but by the fair weather that
you make yourself. It is needful that you frame the 23
season for your own harvest.

DON JOHN   I had rather be a canker in a hedge than a 25
rose in his grace, and it better fits my blood to be dis- 26
dained of all than to fashion a carriage to rob love from 27
any. In this, though I cannot be said to be a flattering
honest man, it must not be denied but I am a plain-
dealing villain. I am trusted with a muzzle and enfran- 30
chised with a clog; therefore I have decreed not to sing 31
in my cage. If I had my mouth, I would bite; if I had
my liberty, I would do my liking. In the meantime let
me be that I am, and seek not to alter me.

CONRADE   Can you make no use of your discontent?

DON JOHN   I make all use of it, for I use it only. Who 36
comes here?

    Enter Borachio.

What news, Borachio?

BORACHIO   I came yonder from a great supper. The

---

11 under Saturn (hence, of a morose disposition)   **11–12 goest . . .
mischief** endeavor to cure with moral commonplaces a deadly disease
14 stomach appetite   **15–16 tend on** attend to   **17 claw** flatter.   **humor**
whim   **19 controlment** restraint   **20 stood out** rebelled   **21 grace**
favor   **23 frame** create   **25 canker** dog rose, one that grows wild rather
than being cultivated in formal gardens   **26 blood** mood, disposition
27 fashion a carriage counterfeit a behavior.   **rob love** gain undeserved
affection   **30 trusted . . . muzzle** i.e., trusted only as far as one trusts a
muzzled animal   **30–31 enfranchised . . . clog** allowed freedom only to
the extent of being hampered by a heavy wooden block   **31 decreed**
determined   **36 for . . . only** it is my only resource

Prince your brother is royally entertained by Leonato,
and I can give you intelligence of an intended mar- 41
riage.

DON JOHN   Will it serve for any model to build mischief 43
on? What is he for a fool that betroths himself to un- 44
quietness?

BORACHIO   Marry, it is your brother's right hand.   46

DON JOHN   Who, the most exquisite Claudio?

BORACHIO   Even he.

DON JOHN   A proper squire! And who, and who? 49
Which way looks he?

BORACHIO   Marry, on Hero, the daughter and heir of
Leonato.

DON JOHN   A very forward March chick! How came you 53
to this?

BORACHIO   Being entertained for a perfumer, as I was 55
smoking a musty room, comes me the Prince and 56
Claudio, hand in hand, in sad conference. I whipped 57
me behind the arras, and there heard it agreed upon 58
that the Prince should woo Hero for himself, and having obtained her, give her to Count Claudio.

DON JOHN   Come, come, let us thither. This may prove
food to my displeasure. That young start-up hath all 62
the glory of my overthrow. If I can cross him any way, 63
I bless myself every way. You are both sure, and will 64
assist me?

CONRADE   To the death, my lord.

DON JOHN   Let us to the great supper. Their cheer is the
greater that I am subdued. Would the cook were o' my 68
mind! Shall we go prove what's to be done? 69

BORACHIO   We'll wait upon your lordship.   *Exeut.*

❖

41 intelligence information   **43 model** design, ground plan   **44 What
. . . fool** what kind of fool is he   **46 Marry** by the Virgin Mary, i.e.,
indeed   **49 proper squire** handsome young man. (Said contemptuously.)   **53 forward March chick** precocious young thing (like a chick
hatched prematurely)   **55 entertained for** hired as   **56 smoking** sweet-
ening the air of (with aromatic smoke).   **comes me** comes. (*Me* is used
colloquially.)   **57 sad** serious   **58 arras** tapestry, hanging   **62 start-up**
upstart   **63 cross** thwart (with allusion, in *bless myself*, to making the
sign of the cross)   **64 sure** trustworthy   **68–69 Would . . . mind** i.e.,
would the cook were of a mind to poison the food   **69 prove** try out

2.1   *Enter Leonato, his brother [Antonio], Hero his*
          daughter, and Beatrice his niece [with Margaret
          and Ursula].

LEONATO   Was not Count John here at supper?

ANTONIO   I saw him not.

BEATRICE   How tartly that gentleman looks! I never can ³
see him but I am heartburned an hour after. ⁴

HERO   He is of a very melancholy disposition.

BEATRICE   He were an excellent man that were made ⁶
just in the midway between him and Benedick. The
one is too like an image and says nothing, and the ⁸
other too like my lady's eldest son, evermore tattling. ⁹

LEONATO   Then half Signor Benedick's tongue in Count
John's mouth, and half Count John's melancholy in
Signor Benedick's face—

BEATRICE   With a good leg and a good foot, uncle, and
money enough in his purse, such a man would win
any woman in the world, if 'a could get her good will. ¹⁵

LEONATO   By my troth, niece, thou wilt never get thee a
husband, if thou be so shrewd of thy tongue. ¹⁷

ANTONIO   In faith, she's too curst. ¹⁸

BEATRICE   Too curst is more than curst. I shall lessen
God's sending that way; for it is said, "God sends a ²⁰
curst cow short horns," but to a cow too curst he sends ²¹
none.

LEONATO   So, by being too curst, God will send you no
horns.

BEATRICE   Just, if he send me no husband, for the which ²⁵
blessing I am at him upon my knees every morning
and evening. Lord, I could not endure a husband with
a beard on his face! I had rather lie in the woolen. ²⁸

LEONATO   You may light on a husband that hath no
beard.

2.1. Location: Leonato's house.
3 tartly sour of disposition   **4 heartburned** afflicted with heartburn or
indigestion   **6 He were** a man would be   **8 image** statue   **9 my . . . son**
i.e., a spoiled child   **15 'a** he   **17 shrewd** sharp   **18 curst** shrewish
20 that way in that respect   **21 curst** i.e., savage, vicious   **25 Just** right,
exactly so   **28 in the woolen** between blankets, without sheets

BEATRICE   What should I do with him? Dress him in my apparel and make him my waiting-gentlewoman? He that hath a beard is more than a youth, and he that hath no beard is less than a man; and he that is more than a youth is not for me, and he that is less than a man, I am not for him. Therefore I will even take sixpence in earnest of the bearward and lead his apes into hell. 37, 38

LEONATO   Well, then, go you into hell?

BEATRICE   No, but to the gate; and there will the devil meet me, like an old cuckold, with horns on his head, and say, "Get you to heaven, Beatrice, get you to heaven, here's no place for you maids." So deliver I up my apes, and away to Saint Peter, for the heavens; he shows me where the bachelors sit, and there live we as merry as the day is long. 44, 45

ANTONIO [*To Hero*]   Well, niece, I trust you will be ruled by your father.

BEATRICE   Yes, faith, it is my cousin's duty to make curtsy and say, "Father, as it please you." But yet for all that, cousin, let him be a handsome fellow, or else make another curtsy and say, "Father, as it please me."

LEONATO   Well, niece, I hope to see you one day fitted with a husband.

BEATRICE   Not till God make men of some other metal than earth. Would it not grieve a woman to be overmastered with a piece of valiant dust? To make an account of her life to a clod of wayward marl? No, uncle, I'll none. Adam's sons are my brethren, and truly I hold it a sin to match in my kindred. 55, 58, 60

LEONATO [*To Hero*]   Daughter, remember what I told you. If the Prince do solicit you in that kind, you know your answer. 62

BEATRICE   The fault will be in the music, cousin, if you

---

37 in earnest in advance payment for.   **bearward** one who keeps and exhibits a bear (and sometimes apes)   **37–38 lead . . . hell** (An ancient proverb says, "Such as die maids do all lead apes in hell.")   **44 for the heavens** (A common interjection, like "By God," but here also carrying its literal meaning, i.e., bound for heaven.)   **45 bachelors** unmarried persons of either sex   **55 metal** substance (with a play on *mettle*)   **58 marl** clay, earth   **60 match . . . kindred** i.e., marry incestuously   **62 in that kind** to that effect (i.e., to marriage)

be not wooed in good time. If the Prince be too impor- 65
tant, tell him there is measure in everything, and so 66
dance out the answer. For, hear me, Hero: wooing,
wedding, and repenting is as a Scotch jig, a measure, 68
and a cinquepace. The first suit is hot and hasty, like 69
a Scotch jig, and full as fantastical; the wedding, man-
nerly-modest, as a measure, full of state and ancientry; 71
and then comes Repentance, and with his bad legs
falls into the cinquepace faster and faster, till he sink
into his grave.

LEONATO Cousin, you apprehend passing shrewdly.   75

BEATRICE I have a good eye, uncle; I can see a church
by daylight.

LEONATO The revelers are entering, brother. Make good
room.   [*The men put on their masks.*]

*Enter [as maskers] Prince [Don] Pedro, Claudio,
and Benedick, and Balthasar, [Borachio,] and
Don John.*

DON PEDRO Lady, will you walk a bout with your 80
friend?   [*The couples pair off for the dance.*] 81

HERO So you walk softly and look sweetly and say
nothing, I am yours for the walk, and especially when
I walk away.

DON PEDRO With me in your company?

HERO I may say so, when I please.

DON PEDRO And when please you to say so?

HERO When I like your favor, for God defend the lute 88
should be like the case!   89

DON PEDRO My visor is Philemon's roof; within the 90
house is Jove.

65 in good time (1) soon (2) in time to the music, rhythmically
65–66 important importunate, urgent **66 measure** (1) moderation
(2) rhythm, dance **68 a measure** a formal dance **69 cinquepace** five-step
lively dance, galliard **71 state and ancientry** dignity and traditional
stateliness **75 apprehend passing shrewdly** understand with unusual
perspicacity **80 walk a bout** take a turn, join in a section of a dance
(here probably a slow, stately pavane) **81 friend** lover of either sex
88 favor face **88–89 God . . . case** i.e., God forbid the face within
should be as unhandsome as its cover, your visor **90 Philemon's roof**
i.e., the humble cottage in which the peasants Philemon and Baucis
entertained Jove, or Jupiter, unawares. (See Ovid, *Metamorphoses*, 8.)

HERO   Why then your visor should be thatched.   92
DON PEDRO   Speak low, if you speak love.
                                    [*They step aside.*]
BALTHASAR   Well, I would you did like me.   94
MARGARET   So would not I for your own sake, for I
  have many ill qualities.
BALTHASAR   Which is one?
MARGARET   I say my prayers aloud.
BALTHASAR   I love you the better. The hearers may cry
  Amen.
MARGARET   God match me with a good dancer!
BALTHASAR   Amen.
MARGARET   And God keep him out of my sight when
  the dance is done! Answer, clerk.   104
BALTHASAR   No more words. The clerk is answered.   105
                                    [*They step aside.*]
URSULA   I know you well enough. You are Signor An-
  tonio.
ANTONIO   At a word, I am not.   108
URSULA   I know you by the waggling of your head.
ANTONIO   To tell you true, I counterfeit him.
URSULA   You could never do him so ill-well unless you   111
  were the very man. Here's his dry hand up and down.   112
  You are he, you are he.
ANTONIO   At a word, I am not.
URSULA   Come, come, do you think I do not know you
  by your excellent wit? Can virtue hide itself? Go to,
  mum, you are he. Graces will appear, and there's an   117
  end.   [*They step aside.*]   118
BEATRICE   Will you not tell me who told you so?
BENEDICK   No, you shall pardon me.
BEATRICE   Nor will you not tell me who you are?
BENEDICK   Not now.
BEATRICE   That I was disdainful and that I had my good

---

92 visor mask.   **thatched** i.e., whiskered, to resemble the thatch of a
humble cottage   **94–105 Balthasar** (The speech prefixes in the quarto
text for Balthasar's lines read *Bene.* and *Balth.*; some editors speculate
that *Borachio* is intended.)   **104 clerk** (So addressed because of Balthasar's repeatedly answering "Amen" like the parish clerk saying the
responses.)   **108 At a word** in short   **111 do . . . ill-well** imitate his
imperfections so perfectly   **112 dry hand** (A sign of age.)   **up and down**
exactly   **117 mum** be silent   **117–118 an end** no more to be said

wit out of the *Hundred Merry Tales*—well, this was 124
Signor Benedick that said so.

BENEDICK   What's he?

BEATRICE   I am sure you know him well enough.

BENEDICK   Not I, believe me.

BEATRICE   Did he never make you laugh?

BENEDICK   I pray you, what is he?

BEATRICE   Why, he is the Prince's jester, a very dull fool.
Only his gift is in devising impossible slanders. None 132
but libertines delight in him, and the commendation 133
is not in his wit but in his villainy, for he both pleases 134
men and angers them, and then they laugh at him and
beat him. I am sure he is in the fleet. I would he had 136
boarded me.   137

BENEDICK   When I know the gentleman, I'll tell him 138
what you say.

BEATRICE   Do, do. He'll but break a comparison or two 140
on me, which peradventure not marked or not laughed 141
at strikes him into melancholy; and then there's a par-
tridge wing saved, for the fool will eat no supper that
night. [*Music.*] We must follow the leaders.   144

BENEDICK   In every good thing.

BEATRICE   Nay, if they lead to any ill, I will leave them
at the next turning.

> *Dance. Exeunt [all except Don John,*
> *Borachio, and Claudio. Don John*
> *and Borachio are unmasked.*]

DON JOHN [*To Borachio*]   Sure my brother is amorous on 148
Hero and hath withdrawn her father to break with
him about it. The ladies follow her, and but one visor
remains.

BORACHIO   And that is Claudio. I know him by his
bearing.

---

124 Hundred Merry Tales (A popular collection of anecdotes first
published by Rastell in 1526.)   **132 Only his gift** his only talent.
impossible incredible   **133 libertines** i.e., those who disregard conventional moral laws   **134 villainy** i.e., mocking, raillery; also,
clownishness   **136 fleet** i.e., crowd, company   **137 boarded** i.e., ac-
costed (continuing the nautical metaphor begun in *fleet*)   **138 know**
become acquainted with   **140 break a comparison** make a scornful
simile or innuendo   **141 peradventure** if it is   **144 leaders** i.e., of the
dance   **148 amorous on** i.e., courting

DON JOHN [*Advancing to Claudio*] Are not you Signor
   Benedick?

CLAUDIO   You know me well. I am he.

DON JOHN   Signor, you are very near my brother in his   157
   love. He is enamored on Hero. I pray you, dissuade   158
   him from her; she is no equal for his birth. You may
   do the part of an honest man in it.

CLAUDIO   How know you he loves her?

DON JOHN   I heard him swear his affection.

BORACHIO   So did I too, and he swore he would marry
   her tonight.

DON JOHN   Come, let us to the banquet.   165

                          Exeunt. Manet Claudio.

CLAUDIO
   Thus answer I in name of Benedick,
   But hear these ill news with the ears of Claudio.
   'Tis certain so. The Prince woos for himself.
   Friendship is constant in all other things
   Save in the office and affairs of love;
   Therefore all hearts in love use their own tongues.   171
   Let every eye negotiate for itself
   And trust no agent; for beauty is a witch
   Against whose charms faith melteth into blood.   174
   This is an accident of hourly proof,   175
   Which I mistrusted not. Farewell therefore Hero!   176

      Enter Benedick [unmasked.]

BENEDICK   Count Claudio?

CLAUDIO   Yea, the same.

BENEDICK   Come, will you go with me?

CLAUDIO   Whither?

BENEDICK   Even to the next willow, about your own   181
   business, County. What fashion will you wear the gar- 182
   land of? About your neck, like an usurer's chain? Or   183
   under your arm, like a lieutenant's scarf? You must   184
   wear it one way, for the Prince hath got your Hero.   185

157–158 near . . . love close to my brother   **165 banquet** light repast of
fruit, wine, and dessert.   **s.d. Manet** he remains onstage   **171 all** i.e., let
all   **174 faith . . . blood** honor gives way to passion   **175 accident** occur-
rence   **176 mistrusted** suspected   **181 willow** (An emblem of disappointed
love.)   **182 County** count   **182–183 garland** i.e., of willow   **184 lieutenant's
scarf** sash worn as a badge of rank   **185 one way** one way or the other

CLAUDIO   I wish him joy of her.

BENEDICK   Why, that's spoken like an honest drovier; so   187
they sell bullocks. But did you think the Prince would   188
have served you thus?

CLAUDIO   I pray you, leave me.

BENEDICK   Ho, now you strike like the blind man. 'Twas   191
the boy that stole your meat, and you'll beat the post.   192

CLAUDIO   If it will not be, I'll leave you.   *Exit.*   193

BENEDICK   Alas, poor hurt fowl! Now will he creep into   194
sedges. But that my Lady Beatrice should know me,   195
and not know me! The Prince's fool! Ha? It may be I
go under that title because I am merry. Yea, but so I
am apt to do myself wrong. I am not so reputed. It is   198
the base, though bitter, disposition of Beatrice that   199
puts the world into her person and so gives me out.   200
Well, I'll be revenged as I may.

Enter the Prince [Don Pedro], Hero, Leonato.
[All are unmasked.]

DON PEDRO   Now, signor, where's the Count? Did you
see him?

BENEDICK   Troth, my lord, I have played the part of Lady   204
Fame. I found him here as melancholy as a lodge in a   205
warren. I told him, and I think I told him true, that   206
Your Grace had got the good will of this young lady,
and I offered him my company to a willow tree, either   208
to make him a garland, as being forsaken, or to bind   209
him up a rod, as being worthy to be whipped.   210

DON PEDRO   To be whipped! What's his fault?

BENEDICK   The flat transgression of a schoolboy, who,   212

---

187 drovier cattle dealer   **188 bullocks** oxen   **191 like the blind man**
(An unidentified allusion to some proverbial story. Cf. the romance
Lazarillo de Tormes, in which the hero steals his master's meat and
revenges himself for the beating he receives by causing the blind man to
jump against a stone pillar.)   **192 post** (1) pillar (2) bearer of news
193 If . . . be i.e., if you won't leave me as I asked   **194–195 creep into
sedges** i.e., hide himself away, as wounded fowl creep into rushes along
the river   **198–200 It is . . . out** it is Beatrice's low and harsh disposition that causes her to attribute to the world her own attitudes and to
represent me accordingly   **204 Troth** by my faith   **204–205 Lady Fame**
Dame Rumor   **205–206 lodge in a warren** isolated gamekeeper's hut in
an enclosure for breeding animals   **208 offered . . . to** offered to accom-
pany him to   **209–210 bind . . . rod** tie several willow switches into a
scourge   **212 flat** plain

being overjoyed with finding a bird's nest, shows it
his companion, and he steals it.

DON PEDRO   Wilt thou make a trust a transgression? The 215
transgression is in the stealer.

BENEDICK   Yet it had not been amiss the rod had been
made, and the garland too; for the garland he might
have worn himself, and the rod he might have bestowed on you, who, as I take it, have stolen his bird's
nest.

DON PEDRO   I will but teach them to sing and restore 222
them to the owner.

BENEDICK   If their singing answer your saying, by my 224
faith, you say honestly.

DON PEDRO   The Lady Beatrice hath a quarrel to you. 226
The gentleman that danced with her told her she is
much wronged by you.

BENEDICK   O, she misused me past the endurance of a 229
block! An oak but with one green leaf on it would 230
have answered her. My very visor began to assume life
and scold with her. She told me, not thinking I had
been myself, that I was the Prince's jester, that I was
duller than a great thaw; huddling jest upon jest with 234
such impossible conveyance upon me that I stood like 235
a man at a mark, with a whole army shooting at me. 236
She speaks poniards, and every word stabs. If her 237
breath were as terrible as her terminations, there were 238
no living near her; she would infect to the North Star. 239
I would not marry her, though she were endowed with
all that Adam had left him before he transgressed. She 241
would have made Hercules have turned spit, yea, and 242
have cleft his club to make the fire too. Come, talk not 243
of her. You shall find her the infernal Ate in good ap- 244

---

215 a trust the act of trusting someone   **222 them** i.e., the young birds in
the nest   **224 answer your saying** correspond to what you say   **226 to**
with   **229 misused** abused   **230 block** (of wood)   **234 great thaw** i.e.,
time when roads are muddy and impassable, obliging one to stay dully at
home.   **huddling** piling, heaping up   **235 impossible conveyance** incredible dexterity   **236 at a mark** at the target   **237 poniards** daggers
238 terminations terms, expressions   **239 North Star** (Supposed the most
remote of stars.)   **241 all . . . him** i.e., Paradise before the fall of man
242 Hercules . . . spit (The Amazon Omphale forced the captive Hercules
to wear women's clothing and spin; turning the spit would be an even
more menial kitchen duty.)   **243 cleft** split   **244 Ate** goddess of discord

parel. I would to God some scholar would conjure her, 245
for certainly, while she is here, a man may live as quiet 246
in hell as in a sanctuary, and people sin upon purpose
because they would go thither; so indeed all disquiet,
horror, and perturbation follows her.

Enter Claudio and Beatrice.

DON PEDRO Look, here she comes.
BENEDICK Will Your Grace command me any service to
the world's end? I will go on the slightest errand now
to the Antipodes that you can devise to send me on; I 253
will fetch you a toothpicker now from the furthest inch 254
of Asia, bring you the length of Prester John's foot, 255
fetch you a hair off the great Cham's beard, do you 256
any embassage to the Pygmies, rather than hold three 257
words' conference with this harpy. You have no em- 258
ployment for me?
DON PEDRO None but to desire your good company.
BENEDICK O God, sir, here's a dish I love not! I cannot
endure my Lady Tongue.   *Exit.*
DON PEDRO Come, lady, come, you have lost the heart
of Signor Benedick.
BEATRICE Indeed, my lord, he lent it me awhile, and I
gave him use for it, a double heart for his single one. 266
Marry, once before he won it of me with false dice;
therefore Your Grace may well say I have lost it.
DON PEDRO You have put him down, lady, you have 269
put him down.
BEATRICE So I would not he should do me, my lord, lest
I should prove the mother of fools. I have brought
Count Claudio, whom you sent me to seek.
DON PEDRO Why, how now, Count? Wherefore are
you sad?

---

245 scholar . . . conjure (Scholars were supposed to be able to conjure
evil spirits back into hell by addressing them in Latin.) **246 here** i.e., on
earth   **253 Antipodes** people and region on the opposite side of the
earth   **254 toothpicker** toothpick   **255 Prester John** a legendary Christian king of the Far East   **256 great Cham** the Khan of Tartary, ruler of
the Mongols   **257 Pygmies** legendary small race thought to live in
India   **258 harpy** legendary creature with a woman's face and body and
a bird's wings and claws   **266 use** usury, interest.   **double** deceitful (?)
269 put him down got the better of him. (But Beatrice plays with
the phrase in its literal sense.)

CLAUDIO   Not sad, my lord.

DON PEDRO   How then? Sick?

CLAUDIO   Neither, my lord.

BEATRICE   The Count is neither sad, nor sick, nor merry,
nor well; but civil count, civil as an orange, and some- 280
thing of that jealous complexion. 281

DON PEDRO   I' faith, lady, I think your blazon to be true, 282
though I'll be sworn, if he be so, his conceit is false. 283
Here, Claudio, I have wooed in thy name, and fair
Hero is won. I have broke with her father and his 285
good will obtained. Name the day of marriage, and
God give thee joy!

LEONATO   Count, take of me my daughter and with her
my fortunes. His Grace hath made the match, and all 289
grace say Amen·to it. 290

BEATRICE   Speak, Count, 'tis your cue.

CLAUDIO   Silence is the perfectest herald of joy. I were
but little happy if I could say how much! Lady, as you
are mine, I am yours. I give away myself for you and
dote upon the exchange.

BEATRICE   Speak, cousin, or if you cannot, stop his
mouth with a kiss, and let not him speak neither.

                    [*Claudio and Hero kiss.*]

DON PEDRO   In faith, lady, you have a merry heart.

BEATRICE   Yea, my lord; I thank it, poor fool, it keeps on
the windy side of care. My cousin tells him in his ear 300
that he is in her heart.

CLAUDIO   And so she doth, cousin.

BEATRICE   Good Lord, for alliance! Thus goes everyone 303
to the world but I, and I am sunburnt. I may sit in a 304
corner and cry, "Heigh-ho for a husband!" 305

DON PEDRO   Lady Beatrice, I will get you one.

---

280 civil serious, grave (punning on *Seville* for the city in Spain whence
came bitter-tasting oranges)   **280–281 something** somewhat   **281 jealous
complexion** i.e., yellow, associated with melancholy and symbolic of jealousy   **282 blazon** description. (A heraldic term.)   **283 conceit** (1) notion,
idea (2) heraldic device (continuing the metaphor of *blazon*)   **285 broke**
spoken   **289–290 all grace** i.e., the source of grace, God   **300 windy** wind-
ward, safe   **303 alliance** relationship by marriage. (Claudio has just called
her "cousin.")   **303–304 goes . . . world** i.e., everyone gets married
304 sunburnt (The Renaissance considered dark complexions unattrac-
tive.)   **305 Heigh-ho . . . husband** (The title of a ballad.)

BEATRICE   I would rather have one of your father's get- 307
ting. Hath Your Grace ne'er a brother like you? Your 308
father got excellent husbands, if a maid could come by
them.

DON PEDRO   Will you have me, lady?

BEATRICE   No, my lord, unless I might have another for
working days. Your Grace is too costly to wear every
day. But I beseech Your Grace, pardon me. I was born
to speak all mirth and no matter.   315

DON PEDRO   Your silence most offends me, and to be
merry best becomes you, for out o' question you
were born in a merry hour.

BEATRICE   No, sure, my lord, my mother cried; but then
there was a star danced, and under that was I born.
Cousins, God give you joy!

LEONATO   Niece, will you look to those things I told
you of?

BEATRICE   I cry you mercy, uncle. [*To Don Pedro.*] 324
By Your Grace's pardon.   *Exit Beatrice.*

DON PEDRO   By my troth, a pleasant-spirited lady.

LEONATO   There's little of the melancholy element in 327
her, my lord. She is never sad but when she sleeps,
and not ever sad then; for I have heard my daughter 329
say, she hath often dreamt of unhappiness and waked
herself with laughing.

DON PEDRO   She cannot endure to hear tell of a husband.

LEONATO   O, by no means. She mocks all her wooers
out of suit.   334

DON PEDRO   She were an excellent wife for Benedick.

LEONATO   O Lord, my lord, if they were but a week
married, they would talk themselves mad.

DON PEDRO   County Claudio, when mean you to go to
church?

CLAUDIO   Tomorrow, my lord. Time goes on crutches
till Love have all his rites.

LEONATO   Not till Monday, my dear son, which is hence

307–308 getting begetting (playing on *get*, "procure," in the previous
speech)   **315 matter** substance   **324 cry you mercy** beg your pardon
(for not having obeyed earlier)   **327 melancholy element** i.e., earth,
associated with the humor of melancholy in the old physiology
329 ever always   **334 out of suit** out of being wooers to her

a just sevennight and a time too brief, too, to have all 343
things answer my mind. 344

DON PEDRO Come, you shake the head at so long a
breathing, but I warrant thee, Claudio, the time shall 346
not go dully by us. I will in the interim undertake one
of Hercules' labors, which is to bring Signor Benedick and the Lady Beatrice into a mountain of affection
th' one with th' other. I would fain have it a match,
and I doubt not but to fashion it, if you three will but
minister such assistance as I shall give you direction. 352

LEONATO My lord, I am for you, though it cost me ten
nights' watchings. 354

CLAUDIO And I, my lord.

DON PEDRO And you too, gentle Hero?

HERO I will do any modest office, my lord, to help my 357
cousin to a good husband.

DON PEDRO And Benedick is not the unhopefullest hus- 359
band that I know. Thus far can I praise him: he is of a
noble strain, of approved valor, and confirmed honesty. 361
I will teach you how to humor your cousin, that she
shall fall in love with Benedick; and I, with your two
helps, will so practice on Benedick that, in despite of
his quick wit and his queasy stomach, he shall fall in 365
love with Beatrice. If we can do this, Cupid is no
longer an archer; his glory shall be ours, for we are the
only love gods. Go in with me, and I will tell you my
drift.   *Exeunt.* 369

❖

2.2   *Enter [Don] John and Borachio.*

DON JOHN It is so. The Count Claudio shall marry the 1
daughter of Leonato.

BORACHIO Yea, my lord, but I can cross it. 3

___

343 a just sevennight exactly a week   **344 answer my mind** suit my
wishes   **346 breathing** pause, interval   **352 minister** furnish, supply
354 watchings staying awake   **357 do . . . office** play any seemly role
359 unhopefullest most unpromising   **361 strain** ancestry.   **approved**
tested.   **honesty** honor   **365 queasy** squeamish, delicate (about marriage)   **369 drift** purpose

2.2. Location: Leonato's house.
1 shall is going to   **3 cross** thwart (also in l. 7)

DON JOHN   Any bar, any cross, any impediment will be 4
medicinable to me. I am sick in displeasure to him, 5
and whatsoever comes athwart his affection ranges 6
evenly with mine. How canst thou cross this mar- 7
riage?

BORACHIO   Not honestly, my lord, but so covertly that
no dishonesty shall appear in me.

DON JOHN   Show me briefly how.

BORACHIO   I think I told your lordship, a year since,
how much I am in the favor of Margaret, the waiting-
gentlewoman to Hero.

DON JOHN   I remember.

BORACHIO   I can, at any unseasonable instant of the 16
night, appoint her to look out at her lady's chamber
window.

DON JOHN   What life is in that, to be the death of this
marriage?

BORACHIO   The poison of that lies in you to temper. Go 21
you to the Prince your brother; spare not to tell him
that he hath wronged his honor in marrying the renowned Claudio—whose estimation do you mightily 24
hold up—to a contaminated stale, such a one as Hero. 25

DON JOHN   What proof shall I make of that?

BORACHIO   Proof enough to misuse the Prince, to vex 27
Claudio, to undo Hero, and kill Leonato. Look you for
any other issue?

DON JOHN   Only to despite them I will endeavor any- 30
thing.

BORACHIO   Go, then, find me a meet hour to draw Don 32
Pedro and the Count Claudio alone. Tell them that you
know that Hero loves me; intend a kind of zeal both 34
to the Prince and Claudio, as—in love of your 35
brother's honor, who hath made this match, and his
friend's reputation, who is thus like to be cozened with 37

---

4 bar obstacle   **5 medicinable** medicinal.   **displeasure to** dislike of
6–7 whatsoever . . . mine whatever crosses his inclination runs parallel
with mine   **16 unseasonable** unsuitable, unseemly   **21 lies in** rests
with.   **temper** mix, compound   **24 estimation** worth   **25 stale** prosti-
tute   **27 misuse** abuse, deceive   **30 despite** torment   **32 meet** suitable   **34 intend** pretend   **35 as** i.e., saying as follows. (The words
between the dashes are to be understood as instructions to Don John as
to what he is to say.)   **37 like** likely.   **cozened** deceived, cheated

the semblance of a maid—that you have discovered 38
thus. They will scarcely believe this without trial. Offer
them instances, which shall bear no less likelihood 40
than to see me at her chamber window, hear me call
Margaret Hero, hear Margaret term me Claudio; and 42
bring them to see this the very night before the intended wedding—for in the meantime I will so fashion the matter that Hero shall be absent—and there
shall appear such seeming truth of Hero's disloyalty
that jealousy shall be called assurance and all the prep- 47
aration overthrown.   48

DON JOHN   Grow this to what adverse issue it can, I will
put it in practice. Be cunning in the working this, and
thy fee is a thousand ducats.   51

BORACHIO   Be you constant in the accusation, and my
cunning shall not shame me.

DON JOHN   I will presently go learn their day of mar- 54
riage.   *Exit [with Borachio].*

✤

2.3   *Enter Benedick alone.*

BENEDICK   Boy!

      [*Enter Boy.*]

BOY   Signor?

BENEDICK   In my chamber window lies a book. Bring it
hither to me in the orchard.   4

BOY   I am here already, sir.   5

BENEDICK   I know that, but I would have thee hence
and here again. *Exit [Boy].* I do much wonder that one
man, seeing how much another man is a fool when he
dedicates his behaviors to love, will, after he hath

---

38 semblance semblance only, outward appearance.   **discovered** revealed   **40 instances** proofs   **42 hear . . . Claudio** (Many editors read
Borachio for *Claudio*. The present reading may be defended if one
imagines that, by arrangement with Margaret, Borachio is playing the
part of *Claudio*, but the reading may also be an inconsistency.)
47 jealousy suspicion.   **assurance** certainty   **47–48 preparation** i.e., for
marriage   **51 ducats** gold coins   **54 presently** immediately

2.3. Location: Leonato's garden.
4 orchard garden   **5 I . . . already** i.e., I will be so quick as to use no
time at all. (But Benedick quibbles on the literal sense.)

laughed at such shallow follies in others, become the
argument of his own scorn by falling in love; and such 11
a man is Claudio. I have known when there was no 12
music with him but the drum and the fife, and now 13
had he rather hear the tabor and the pipe. I have 14
known when he would have walked ten mile afoot to
see a good armor, and now will he lie ten nights 16
awake carving the fashion of a new doublet. He was 17
wont to speak plain and to the purpose, like an honest
man and a soldier, and now is he turned orthogra- 19
phy—his words are a very fantastical banquet, just so 20
many strange dishes. May I be so converted and see
with these eyes? I cannot tell; I think not. I will not be
sworn but Love may transform me to an oyster, but I'll
take my oath on it, till he have made an oyster of me,
he shall never make me such a fool. One woman is
fair, yet I am well; another is wise, yet I am well; another virtuous, yet I am well; but till all graces be in
one woman, one woman shall not come in my grace.
Rich she shall be, that's certain; wise, or I'll none; vir- 29
tuous, or I'll never cheapen her; fair, or I'll never look 30
on her; mild, or come not near me; noble, or not I for 31
an angel; of good discourse, an excellent musician, 32
and her hair shall be of what color it please God.
Ha! The Prince and Monsieur Love! I will hide me in
the arbor.   [*He withdraws.*]

Enter Prince [Don Pedro], Leonato, Claudio.

DON PEDRO   Come, shall we hear this music?

CLAUDIO
Yea, my good lord. How still the evening is,
As hushed on purpose to grace harmony!   38
DON PEDRO [*Aside to them*]
See you where Benedick hath hid himself?

---

11 **argument** subject   12–13 **there was . . . fife** i.e., his only commitment
was to soldiering   14 **tabor . . . pipe** (Symbols of peaceful merriment.)
16 **armor** suit of armor   17 **carving** planning.   **doublet** jacket
19–20 **turned orthography** become fastidious and fashionable in his
choice of language   29 **I'll none** I'll have none of her   30 **cheapen** ask
the price of, bid for   31, 32 **noble, angel** (Each of these words involves a
pun on the meaning "a coin," a noble being worth 6 shillings 8 pence
and an angel 10 shillings.)   38 **grace harmony** do honor to music

CLAUDIO [*Aside in reply*]
　　O, very well, my lord. The music ended,　　　　　　40
　　We'll fit the kid-fox with a pennyworth.　　　　　　41

　　Enter Balthasar with Music.

DON PEDRO
　　Come, Balthasar, we'll hear that song again.
BALTHASAR
　　O good my lord, tax not so bad a voice
　　To slander music any more than once.
DON PEDRO
　　It is the witness still of excellency　　　　　　　　45
　　To put a strange face on his own perfection.　　　　46
　　I pray thee, sing, and let me woo no more.　　　　　47
BALTHASAR
　　Because you talk of wooing, I will sing,
　　Since many a wooer doth commence his suit
　　To her he thinks not worthy, yet he woos,
　　Yet will he swear he loves.
DON PEDRO　　　　　　　　Nay, pray thee, come,
　　Or if thou wilt hold longer argument,
　　Do it in notes.
BALTHASAR　　　　Note this before my notes:　　　　53
　　There's not a note of mine that's worth the noting.
DON PEDRO
　　Why, these are very crotchets that he speaks!　　　55
　　Note, notes, forsooth, and nothing.　　[*Music.*]　56
BENEDICK　Now, divine air! Now is his soul ravished! Is　57
　　it not strange that sheeps' guts should hale souls out of　58
　　men's bodies? Well, a horn for my money, when all's　59
　　done.

---

40 The music ended when the music is over　**41 We'll . . . pennyworth**
i.e., we'll give our sly victim more than he bargained for. (Benedick is
called *kid-fox*, a term from beast fable, because he is sly like a fox and
is being duped in their game like a kid.)　**45–46 It . . . perfection** it is
always characteristic of excellence to pretend not to know its own
skill　**47 woo** entreat　**53 notes** music　**55 crotchets** (1) whim, fancy
(2) musical notes of brief duration　**56 nothing** (With a pun on *noting;* the
two words were pronounced alike. Cf. the same pun in the title of the
play, where *Nothing* suggests "noting," or eavesdropping.)　**57 air**
melody　**58 sheeps' guts** strings on musical instruments.　**hale** draw
59 a horn a hunting horn, a more masculine instrument than a fiddle.
(But with a perhaps unconscious allusion to a cuckold's horns.)

The Song.

BALTHASAR

Sigh no more, ladies, sigh no more,
  Men were deceivers ever,
One foot in sea and one on shore,
  To one thing constant never.
Then sigh not so, but let them go,
  And be you blithe and bonny,   66
Converting all your sounds of woe
  Into Hey nonny, nonny.   68

Sing no more ditties, sing no moe,   69
  Of dumps so dull and heavy;   70
The fraud of men was ever so,
  Since summer first was leavy.   72
Then sigh not so, but let them go,
  And be you blithe and bonny,
Converting all your sounds of woe
  Into Hey nonny, nonny.

DON PEDRO   By my troth, a good song.

BALTHASAR   And an ill singer, my lord.

DON PEDRO   Ha, no, no, faith, thou sing'st well enough
for a shift.   80

BENEDICK [*Aside*]   An he had been a dog that should 81
have howled thus, they would have hanged him, and
I pray God his bad voice bode no mischief. I had as
lief have heard the night raven, come what plague 84
could have come after it.

DON PEDRO   Yea, marry, dost thou hear, Balthasar? I 86
pray thee, get us some excellent music, for tomorrow
night we would have it at the Lady Hero's chamber
window.

BALTHASAR   The best I can, my lord.

---

66 blithe and bonny cheerful and joyful   **68 Hey nonny, nonny** (A nonsense refrain.)   **69 moe** more   **70 dumps** mournful songs; also, dances   **72 leavy** leafy   **80 for a shift** in a pinch   **81 An** if (also in l. 161)   **84 lief** willingly.   **night raven** some bird of night, portending disaster   **86 Yea, marry** (A continuation of Don Pedro's speech preceding Benedick's aside.)

DON PEDRO Do so. Farewell. (*Exit Balthasar.*) Come
  hither, Leonato. What was it you told me of today,
  that your niece Beatrice was in love with Signor Benedick?

CLAUDIO O, ay! [*Aside to Pedro.*] Stalk on, stalk on; the 95
  fowl sits.—I did never think that lady would have 96
  loved any man.

LEONATO No, nor I neither, but most wonderful that
  she should so dote on Signor Benedick, whom she
  hath in all outward behaviors seemed ever to abhor.

BENEDICK [*Aside*] Is 't possible? Sits the wind in that 101
  corner? 102

LEONATO By my troth, my lord, I cannot tell what to
  think of it but that she loves him with an enraged af- 104
  fection; it is past the infinite of thought. 105

DON PEDRO Maybe she doth but counterfeit.

CLAUDIO Faith, like enough. 107

LEONATO O God, counterfeit? There was never counterfeit of passion came so near the life of passion as she
  discovers it. 110

DON PEDRO Why, what effects of passion shows she?

CLAUDIO [*Aside to them*] Bait the hook well; this
  fish will bite.

LEONATO What effects, my lord? She will sit you—you 114
  heard my daughter tell you how.

CLAUDIO She did indeed.

DON PEDRO How, how, I pray you? You amaze me. I
  would have thought her spirit had been invincible
  against all assaults of affection.

LEONATO I would have sworn it had, my lord—especially against Benedick.

BENEDICK [*Aside*] I should think this a gull but that the 122
  white-bearded fellow speaks it. Knavery cannot, sure,
  hide himself in such reverence.

CLAUDIO [*Aside to them*] He hath ta'en th' infection.
  Hold it up. 126

95–96 Stalk . . . sits i.e., proceed stealthily; the hunted bird is hiding in
the bush **101–102 Sits . . . corner** is that the way the wind is blowing?
(i.e., is that how things are?) **104 enraged** maddened with passion
105 infinite farthest reach **107 like** likely **110 discovers** betrays
114 sit you i.e., sit. (*You* is used idiomatically.) **122 gull** trick, deception. **but** except for the fact **126 Hold it up** keep up the jest

DON PEDRO   Hath she made her affection known to Benedick?

LEONATO   No, and swears she never will. That's her torment.

CLAUDIO   'Tis true, indeed. So your daughter says. "Shall I," says she, "that have so oft encountered him 132 with scorn, write to him that I love him?"

LEONATO   This says she now when she is beginning to write to him, for she'll be up twenty times a night, and there will she sit in her smock till she have writ a sheet 136 of paper. My daughter tells us all.

CLAUDIO   Now you talk of a sheet of paper, I remember a pretty jest your daughter told us of.

LEONATO   O, when she had writ it and was reading it over, she found "Benedick" and "Beatrice" between the sheet?

CLAUDIO   That. 143

LEONATO   O, she tore the letter into a thousand half- 144 pence; railed at herself, that she should be so immodest 145 to write to one that she knew would flout her. "I mea- 146 sure him," says she, "by my own spirit, for I should flout him, if he writ to me. Yea, though I love him, I should."

CLAUDIO   Then down upon her knees she falls, weeps, sobs, beats her heart, tears her hair, prays, curses: "O sweet Benedick! God give me patience!"

LEONATO   She doth indeed; my daughter says so. And the ecstasy hath so much overborne her that my 154 daughter is sometimes afeard she will do a desperate outrage to herself. It is very true.

DON PEDRO   It were good that Benedick knew of it by some other, if she will not discover it. 158

CLAUDIO   To what end? He would make but a sport of it and torment the poor lady worse.

DON PEDRO   An he should, it were an alms to hang him. 161 She's an excellent sweet lady, and, out of all suspicion, 162 she is virtuous.

CLAUDIO   And she is exceeding wise.

---

132 she i.e., Beatrice 136 smock chemise 143 That i.e., that's it
144–145 halfpence i.e., small pieces 146 flout mock 154 overborne overwhelmed 158 discover reveal 161 alms good deed 162 out of beyond

DON PEDRO   In everything but in loving Benedick.

LEONATO   O my lord, wisdom and blood combating in 166
so tender a body, we have ten proofs to one that blood
hath the victory. I am sorry for her, as I have just
cause, being her uncle and her guardian.

DON PEDRO   I would she had bestowed this dotage on 170
me. I would have doffed all other respects and made 171
her half myself. I pray you, tell Benedick of it, and hear 172
what 'a will say.

LEONATO   Were it good, think you?

CLAUDIO   Hero thinks surely she will die; for she says
she will die if he love her not, and she will die ere she
make her love known, and she will die if he woo her,
rather than she will bate one breath of her accustomed 178
crossness. 179

DON PEDRO   She doth well. If she should make tender of 180
her love, 'tis very possible he'll scorn it; for the man,
as you know all, hath a contemptible spirit. 182

CLAUDIO   He is a very proper man. 183

DON PEDRO   He hath indeed a good outward happiness. 184

CLAUDIO   Before God, and in my mind, very wise.

DON PEDRO   He doth indeed show some sparks that are
like wit.

CLAUDIO   And I take him to be valiant.

DON PEDRO   As Hector, I assure you; and in the man- 189
aging of quarrels you may say he is wise, for either he
avoids them with great discretion or undertakes them
with a most Christian-like fear.

LEONATO   If he do fear God, 'a must necessarily keep
peace. If he break the peace, he ought to enter into a
quarrel with fear and trembling.

DON PEDRO   And so will he do, for the man doth fear
God, howsoever it seems not in him by some large 197
jests he will make. Well, I am sorry for your niece.
Shall we go seek Benedick, and tell him of her love?

---

166 blood natural feeling   **170 dotage** doting affection   **171 doffed** put
or turned aside.   **respects** considerations   **172 half myself** i.e., my
wife   **178 bate** abate   **179 crossness** perversity, contrariety   **180 tender**
offer   **182 contemptible** contemptuous   **183 proper** handsome
184 outward happiness fortune in his good looks   **189 Hector** the
mightiest of the Trojans   **197 by** to judge by.   **large** broad, indelicate

CLAUDIO Never tell him, my lord. Let her wear it out 200
with good counsel. 201

LEONATO Nay, that's impossible. She may wear her
heart out first.

DON PEDRO Well, we will hear further of it by your
daughter. Let it cool the while. I love Benedick well,
and I could wish he would modestly examine himself,
to see how much he is unworthy so good a lady.

LEONATO My lord, will you walk? Dinner is ready.

                           [*They walk aside.*]

CLAUDIO If he do not dote on her upon this, I will never
trust my expectation.

DON PEDRO Let there be the same net spread for her,
and that must your daughter and her gentlewomen
carry. The sport will be when they hold one an opin- 213
ion of another's dotage, and no such matter; that's the 214
scene that I would see, which will be merely a dumb 215
show. Let us send her to call him in to dinner. 216

          [*Exeunt Don Pedro, Claudio, and Leonato.*]

BENEDICK [*Coming forward*] This can be no trick. The
conference was sadly borne. They have the truth of 218
this from Hero. They seem to pity the lady. It seems
her affections have their full bent. Love me? Why, it 220
must be requited. I hear how I am censured. They say
I will bear myself proudly, if I perceive the love come
from her; they say too that she will rather die than give
any sign of affection. I did never think to marry. I must
not seem proud; happy are they that hear their detrac- 225
tions and can put them to mending. They say the lady 226
is fair; 'tis a truth, I can bear them witness; and virtuous; 'tis so, I cannot reprove it; and wise but for 228
loving me; by my troth, it is no addition to her wit,
nor no great argument of her folly, for I will be horribly
in love with her. I may chance have some odd quirks 231

---

200 wear it out eradicate it   **201 counsel** reflection, deliberation
213–214 they . . . dotage each believes the other to be in love   **214 no
such matter** the reality is quite otherwise   **215–216 dumb show** panto-
mime (lacking their usual banter)   **218 sadly borne** soberly conducted
220 have . . . bent i.e., are fully engaged. (The image is of a bow pulled
taut.)   **225–226 their detractions** criticisms of themselves   **226 put . . .
mending** undertake to remedy the defect   **228 reprove** refute   **231
quirks** witty conceits or jokes

and remnants of wit broken on me, because I have
railed so long against marriage. But doth not the appetite alter? A man loves the meat in his youth that he
cannot endure in his age. Shall quips and sentences   235
and these paper bullets of the brain awe a man from   236
the career of his humor? No, the world must be peo-   237
pled. When I said I would die a bachelor, I did not
think I should live till I were married. Here comes Beatrice. By this day, she's a fair lady! I do spy some
marks of love in her.

    Enter Beatrice.

BEATRICE   Against my will I am sent to bid you come in
  to dinner.
BENEDICK   Fair Beatrice, I thank you for your pains.
BEATRICE   I took no more pains for those thanks than
  you take pains to thank me. If it had been painful, I
  would not have come.
BENEDICK   You take pleasure then in the message?
BEATRICE   Yea, just so much as you may take upon a   249
  knife's point and choke a daw withal. You have no   250
  stomach, signor. Fare you well.   *Exit.*   251
BENEDICK   Ha! "Against my will I am sent to bid you
  come in to dinner." There's a double meaning in that.
  "I took no more pains for those thanks than you took
  pains to thank me." That's as much as to say, "Any
  pains that I take for you is as easy as thanks." If I do
  not take pity of her, I am a villain; if I do not love her,
  I am a Jew. I will go get her picture.   *Exit.*

❖

---

235 quips sharp or sarcastic remarks. **sentences** saws, maxims **236
paper bullets** i.e., words **237 career of his humor** pursuit of his inclination **249–250 just . . . withal** i.e., very little. (A daw or jackdaw is a
common blackbird, smaller than a crow.) **251 stomach** appetite

3.1   *Enter Hero and two gentlewomen, Margaret and Ursula.*

HERO
Good Margaret, run thee to the parlor.
There shalt thou find my cousin Beatrice
Proposing with the Prince and Claudio.   3
Whisper her ear and tell her I and Ursley   4
Walk in the orchard, and our whole discourse
Is all of her. Say that thou overheardst us,
And bid her steal into the pleachèd bower   7
Where honeysuckles, ripened by the sun,
Forbid the sun to enter—like favorites
Made proud by princes, that advance their pride   10
Against that power that bred it. There will she hide her 11
To listen our propose. This is thy office.   12
Bear thee well in it and leave us alone.   13
MARGARET
I'll make her come, I warrant you, presently.   [*Exit.*] 14
HERO
Now, Ursula, when Beatrice doth come,
As we do trace this alley up and down   16
Our talk must only be of Benedick.
When I do name him, let it be thy part
To praise him more than ever man did merit.
My talk to thee must be how Benedick
Is sick in love with Beatrice. Of this matter
Is little Cupid's crafty arrow made,
That only wounds by hearsay.

   Enter Beatrice [behind].

                              Now begin,   23
For look where Beatrice, like a lapwing, runs   24
Close by the ground to hear our conference.

3.1. Location: Leonato's garden.
3 Proposing conversing   **4 Ursley** (A nickname for *Ursula*.)   **7 pleachèd**
formed by densely interwoven branches   **10–11 that . . . it** i.e., who dare
set themselves up against the very princes who advanced them   **12 listen our propose** listen to our conversation.   **office** responsibility
13 leave us alone leave the rest to us   **14 presently** immediately
16 trace walk   **23 only . . . hearsay** wounds by mere report   **24 lapwing**
bird of the plover family

URSULA [*Aside to Hero*]
　The pleasant'st angling is to see the fish
　Cut with her golden oars the silver stream   27
　And greedily devour the treacherous bait.
　So angle we for Beatrice, who even now
　Is couchèd in the woodbine coverture.   30
　Fear you not my part of the dialogue.
HERO [*Aside to Ursula*]
　Then go we near her, that her ear lose nothing
　Of the false sweet bait that we lay for it.
　　　　　　　　　　[*They approach the bower.*]
　No, truly, Ursula, she is too disdainful;
　I know her spirits are as coy and wild   35
　As haggards of the rock.
URSULA　　　　　　　　But are you sure   36
　That Benedick loves Beatrice so entirely?
HERO
　So says the Prince and my new-trothèd lord.
URSULA
　And did they bid you tell her of it, madam?
HERO
　They did entreat me to acquaint her of it;
　But I persuaded them, if they loved Benedick,
　To wish him wrestle with affection
　And never to let Beatrice know of it.
URSULA
　Why did you so? Doth not the gentleman
　Deserve as full as fortunate a bed   45
　As ever Beatrice shall couch upon?   46
HERO
　O god of love! I know he doth deserve
　As much as may be yielded to a man;
　But Nature never framed a woman's heart
　Of prouder stuff than that of Beatrice.
　Disdain and scorn ride sparkling in her eyes,
　Misprizing what they look on, and her wit   52

---

27 oars i.e., fins　**30 woodbine coverture** bower, or arbor, of honey-
suckle　**35 coy** disdainful　**36 haggards** untamed female hawks.　**rock**
i.e., mountainous terrain　**45–46 as full . . . upon** i.e., as good a wife as
Beatrice　**52 Misprizing** undervaluing

Values itself so highly that to her
All matter else seems weak. She cannot love,   54
Nor take no shape nor project of affection,   55
She is so self-endearèd.

URSULA   Sure I think so,   56
And therefore certainly it were not good
She knew his love, lest she'll make sport at it.

HERO
Why, you speak truth. I never yet saw man,
How wise, how noble, young, how rarely featured,   60
But she would spell him backward. If fair-faced,   61
She would swear the gentleman should be her sister;
If black, why, Nature, drawing of an antic,   63
Made a foul blot; if tall, a lance ill-headed;
If low, an agate very vilely cut;   65
If speaking, why, a vane blown with all winds;
If silent, why, a block movèd with none.
So turns she every man the wrong side out
And never gives to truth and virtue that
Which simpleness and merit purchaseth.   70

URSULA
Sure, sure, such carping is not commendable.

HERO
No, not to be so odd and from all fashions   72
As Beatrice is cannot be commendable.
But who dare tell her so? If I should speak,
She would mock me into air; O, she would laugh me
Out of myself, press me to death with wit.   76
Therefore let Benedick, like covered fire,
Consume away in sighs, waste inwardly.   78
It were a better death than die with mocks,
Which is as bad as die with tickling.

---

54 weak unimportant   **55 project** conception, idea   **56 self-endearèd** full of self-love   **60 How** however.   **rarely** excellently   **61 spell him backward** i.e., speak contrarily of him by characterizing his virtues as vices **63 black** dark.   **antic** buffoon, grotesque figure   **65 agate** i.e., diminutive person (alluding to the small figures cut in agate for rings)   **70 simpleness** integrity, plainness   **72 from** contrary to   **76 press me to death** (Pressing to death with weights was the usual punishment for those accused of crimes who refused to plead either guilty or not guilty.)   **78 Consume . . . sighs** (An allusion to the belief that each sigh cost the heart a drop of blood.)

URSULA
  Yet tell her of it. Hear what she will say.
HERO
  No, rather I will go to Benedick
  And counsel him to fight against his passion.
  And truly, I'll devise some honest slanders   84
  To stain my cousin with. One doth not know
  How much an ill word may empoison liking.
URSULA
  O, do not do your cousin such a wrong!
  She cannot be so much without true judgment—
  Having so swift and excellent a wit
  As she is prized to have—as to refuse   90
  So rare a gentleman as Signor Benedick.
HERO
  He is the only man of Italy,
  Always excepted my dear Claudio.
URSULA
  I pray you, be not angry with me, madam,
  Speaking my fancy: Signor Benedick,
  For shape, for bearing, argument, and valor,   96
  Goes foremost in report through Italy.
HERO
  Indeed, he hath an excellent good name.
URSULA
  His excellence did earn it, ere he had it.
  When are you married, madam?
HERO
  Why, every day, tomorrow. Come, go in.   101
  I'll show thee some attires and have thy counsel
  Which is the best to furnish me tomorrow.
                              [*They walk away.*]
URSULA [*Aside to Hero*]
  She's limed, I warrant you. We have caught her, madam.   104
HERO [*Aside to Ursula*]
  If it prove so, then loving goes by haps;   105

---

84 honest slanders i.e., slanders that do not involve her virtue
90 prized esteemed   **96 argument** skill in discourse   **101 every day,
tomorrow** tomorrow and every day thereafter   **104 limed** caught, like a
bird in birdlime, a sticky substance spread on branches to trap the
birds that perch on them   **105 by haps** by chance

Some Cupid kills with arrows, some with traps.
                         [*Exeunt Hero and Ursula.*]
BEATRICE [*Coming forward*]
  What fire is in mine ears? Can this be true?   107
    Stand I condemned for pride and scorn so much?
  Contempt, farewell, and maiden pride, adieu!
    No glory lives behind the back of such.   110
  And Benedick, love on; I will requite thee,
    Taming my wild heart to thy loving hand.   112
  If thou dost love, my kindness shall incite thee
    To bind our loves up in a holy band;   114
  For others say thou dost deserve, and I
  Believe it better than reportingly.   *Exit.* 116

❖

3.2   *Enter Prince [Don Pedro], Claudio, Benedick,*
       and Leonato.

DON PEDRO I do but stay till your marriage be consum- 1
  mate, and then go I toward Aragon. 2
CLAUDIO I'll bring you thither, my lord, if you'll vouch- 3
  safe me. 4
DON PEDRO Nay, that would be as great a soil in the 5
  new gloss of your marriage as to show a child his new
  coat and forbid him to wear it. I will only be bold with 7
  Benedick for his company, for from the crown of his
  head to the sole of his foot he is all mirth. He hath
  twice or thrice cut Cupid's bowstring, and the little
  hangman dare not shoot at him. He hath a heart as 11
  sound as a bell, and his tongue is the clapper, for what
  his heart thinks his tongue speaks.

107 What . . . ears (An allusion to the old saying that a person's ears
burn when one is being discussed in one's absence.)   **110 No . . . such**
no good is spoken of such persons when their backs are turned
112 Taming . . . hand (A figure derived from the taming of the hawk by
the hand of the falconer.)   **114 band** bond   **116 better than reportingly**
on better evidence than mere report

3.2. Location: Leonato's house.
1–2 consummate consummated   **3 bring** escort   **3–4 vouchsafe** allow
5 soil stain   **7 be bold with** ask   **11 hangman** executioner; rogue.
(Playfully applied to Cupid.)

BENEDICK Gallants, I am not as I have been.

LEONATO So say I. Methinks you are sadder.   15

CLAUDIO I hope he be in love.

DON PEDRO Hang him, truant! There's no true drop of blood in him, to be truly touched with love. If he be sad, he wants money.

BENEDICK I have the toothache.   20

DON PEDRO Draw it.   21

BENEDICK Hang it!   22

CLAUDIO You must hang it first and draw it afterwards.

DON PEDRO What, sigh for the toothache?

LEONATO Where is but a humor or a worm.   26

BENEDICK Well, everyone can master a grief but he that has it.   27

CLAUDIO Yet say I, he is in love.

DON PEDRO There is no appearance of fancy in him, unless it be a fancy that he hath to strange disguises; as, to be a Dutchman today, a Frenchman tomorrow, or in the shape of two countries at once, as, a German from the waist downward, all slops, and a Spaniard from the hip upward, no doublet. Unless he have a fancy to this foolery, as it appears he hath, he is no fool for fancy, as you would have it appear he is.   30 31 34 35 37

CLAUDIO If he be not in love with some woman, there is no believing old signs. 'A brushes his hat o' mornings. What should that bode?

DON PEDRO Hath any man seen him at the barber's?

CLAUDIO No, but the barber's man hath been seen with him, and the old ornament of his cheek hath already stuffed tennis balls.   43 44

---

15 **sadder** more serious 20 **toothache** (Thought to be a common ailment of lovers.) 21 **Draw** extract. (But Claudio jokes on the method of executing traitors, who were hanged first and then cut down alive and drawn, i.e., disemboweled, and finally quartered.) 22 **Hang it** confound it 26 **Where** where there. **humor or a worm** (Toothache was ascribed to "humors," or unhealthy secretions, and to actual worms in the teeth.) 27 **but** except 30–31 **fancy . . . fancy** love . . . whim, liking 34 **slops** loose breeches 35 **no doublet** i.e., with a hip-length cloak in place of the close-fitting doublet 37 **fool for fancy** i.e., lover 43–44 **old . . . tennis balls** i.e., Benedick's beard has gone to stuff tennis balls. (He appears onstage beardless in this scene for the first time.)

LEONATO   Indeed he looks younger than he did, by the loss of a beard.

DON PEDRO   Nay, 'a rubs himself with civet. Can you 47 smell him out by that?

CLAUDIO   That's as much as to say, the sweet youth's in love.

DON PEDRO   The greatest note of it is his melancholy. 51

CLAUDIO   And when was he wont to wash his face? 52

DON PEDRO   Yea, or to paint himself? For the which I hear what they say of him.

CLAUDIO   Nay, but his jesting spirit, which is now crept into a lute string and now governed by stops. 56

DON PEDRO   Indeed, that tells a heavy tale for him. Conclude, conclude he is in love.

CLAUDIO   Nay, but I know who loves him.

DON PEDRO   That would I know too. I warrant, one that knows him not.

CLAUDIO   Yes, and his ill conditions; and, in despite of 62 all, dies for him.

DON PEDRO   She shall be buried with her face upwards. 64

BENEDICK   Yet is this no charm for the toothache. Old signor, walk aside with me. I have studied eight or nine wise words to speak to you, which these hobby- 67 horses must not hear. [*Exeunt Benedick and Leonato.*] 68

DON PEDRO   For my life, to break with him about Beatrice. 69

CLAUDIO   'Tis even so. Hero and Margaret have by this 71 played their parts with Beatrice, and then the two bears will not bite one another when they meet.

    Enter [Don] John the Bastard.

DON JOHN   My lord and brother, God save you!

---

47 civet perfume derived from the civet cat   **51 note** mark   **52 wash** i.e., with cosmetics; similarly with *paint* in the next line   **56 stops** (1) frets on the fingerboard (2) restraints   **62 ill conditions** bad qualities **64 buried . . . upwards** i.e., as the faithful, not as a suicide, who were sometimes buried face downwards (?). (Probably there is also a ribald suggestion, continuing the joke on *dies for him* meaning to make love.)   **67–68 hobbyhorses** i.e., buffoons. (Originally figures in a morris dance made to resemble a horse and rider.)   **69 For** upon.   **break** speak   **71 Margaret** (Ursula joined Hero in playing the trick on Beatrice, but Margaret has been in on it.)

DON PEDRO Good e'en, brother.   75

DON JOHN If your leisure served, I would speak with
you.

DON PEDRO In private?

DON JOHN If it please you. Yet Count Claudio may hear,
for what I would speak of concerns him.

DON PEDRO What's the matter?

DON JOHN [*To Claudio*] Means your lordship to be married tomorrow?

DON PEDRO You know he does.

DON JOHN I know not that, when he knows what I
know.

CLAUDIO If there be any impediment, I pray you dis-   87
cover it.   88

DON JOHN You may think I love you not. Let that appear hereafter, and aim better at me by that I now will   90
manifest. For my brother, I think he holds you well   91
and in dearness of heart hath holp to effect your en-   92
suing marriage—surely suit ill spent and labor ill bestowed.

DON PEDRO Why, what's the matter?

DON JOHN I came hither to tell you, and, circumstances   96
shortened, for she has been too long a-talking of, the   97
lady is disloyal.

CLAUDIO Who, Hero?

DON JOHN Even she—Leonato's Hero, your Hero,
every man's Hero.

CLAUDIO Disloyal?

DON JOHN The word is too good to paint out her   103
wickedness. I could say she were worse; think you of
a worse title, and I will fit her to it. Wonder not till   105
further warrant. Go but with me tonight, you shall see   106
her chamber window entered, even the night before
her wedding day. If you love her then, tomorrow wed
her; but it would better fit your honor to change your
mind.

CLAUDIO May this be so?

---

75 e'en evening, i.e., afternoon **87–88 discover** reveal **90 aim better at**
judge better of. **that** that which **91 holds you well** thinks well of
you **92 holp** helped **96–97 circumstances shortened** without unnecessary details **97 a-talking of** under discussion (by us) **103 paint out**
portray in full **105–106 till further warrant** till further proof appears

DON PEDRO   I will not think it.

DON JOHN   If you dare not trust that you see, confess not   113
that you know. If you will follow me, I will show you   114
enough; and when you have seen more and heard
more, proceed accordingly.

CLAUDIO   If I see anything tonight why I should not
marry her, tomorrow in the congregation, where I
should wed, there will I shame her.

DON PEDRO   And, as I wooed for thee to obtain her, I will
join with thee to disgrace her.

DON JOHN   I will disparage her no farther till you are my
witnesses. Bear it coldly but till midnight, and let the   123
issue show itself.

DON PEDRO   O day untowardly turned!   125

CLAUDIO   O mischief strangely thwarting!

DON JOHN   O plague right well prevented! So will you
say when you have seen the sequel.   [*Exeunt.*]

❖

3.3   *Enter Dogberry and his compartner* [*Verges*]
with the Watch.

DOGBERRY   Are you good men and true?

VERGES   Yea, or else it were pity but they should suffer
salvation, body and soul.   3

DOGBERRY   Nay, that were a punishment too good for
them, if they should have any allegiance in them,   5
being chosen for the Prince's watch.

VERGES   Well, give them their charge, neighbor Dog-   7
berry.

DOGBERRY   First, who think you the most desartless   9
man to be constable?

FIRST WATCH   Hugh Oatcake, sir, or George Seacoal, for
they can write and read.

113–114 If . . . know i.e., when you have seen what I'll show you, either
admit that what you know is true or admit that you're denying a
certainty   **123 coldly** calmly   **125 untowardly turned** perversely
altered

3.3. Location: A street.
3 salvation (A blunder for *damnation*.)   **5 allegiance** (For *treachery*.)
7 charge instructions   **9 desartless** (For *deserving*.)

DOGBERRY   Come hither, neighbor Seacoal. [*Seacoal, or
Second Watch, steps forward.*] God hath blessed you
with a good name. To be a well-favored man is the gift 15
of fortune, but to write and read comes by nature.

SEACOAL   Both which, Master Constable—

DOGBERRY   You have. I knew it would be your answer.
Well, for your favor, sir, why, give God thanks, and
make no boast of it; and for your writing and reading,
let that appear when there is no need of such vanity.
You are thought here to be the most senseless and fit 22
man for the constable of the watch; therefore bear you
the lantern. This is your charge: you shall comprehend 24
all vagrom men; you are to bid any man stand, in the 25
Prince's name.

SEACOAL   How if 'a will not stand?

DOGBERRY   Why, then, take no note of him, but let him
go, and presently call the rest of the watch together
and thank God you are rid of a knave.

VERGES   If he will not stand when he is bidden, he is
none of the Prince's subjects.

DOGBERRY   True, and they are to meddle with none but
the Prince's subjects. You shall also make no noise in
the streets; for, for the watch to babble and to talk is
most tolerable and not to be endured.   36

WATCH   We will rather sleep than talk. We know what 37
belongs to a watch.   38

DOGBERRY   Why, you speak like an ancient and most
quiet watchman, for I cannot see how sleeping should
offend. Only have a care that your bills be not stolen. 41
Well, you are to call at all the alehouses and bid those
that are drunk get them to bed.

WATCH   How if they will not?

DOGBERRY   Why, then, let them alone till they are sober.

---

15 a good name (Sea coal was high-grade coal shipped from Newcastle,
not the charcoal usually sold by London colliers.)   **well-favored** good-
looking   **22 senseless** (For *sensible*.)   **24 comprehend** (For *apprehend*.)
25 vagrom vagrant.   **stand** stand still, stop   **36 tolerable** (For *intolera-
ble*.)   **37 s.p. Watch** (Here and at ll. 44, 48, 53, and 66 Shakespeare's text
does not specify which watchman speaks. These lines are sometimes
assigned to the Second Watch, Seacoal, but could be spoken by others
of the watch.)   **38 belongs to** are the duties of   **41 bills** pikes, with axes
fixed to long poles

If they make you not then the better answer, you may
say they are not the men you took them for.

WATCH   Well, sir.

DOGBERRY   If you meet a thief, you may suspect him,
by virtue of your office, to be no true man; and for   50
such kind of men, the less you meddle or make with   51
them, why, the more is for your honesty.   52

WATCH   If we know him to be a thief, shall we not lay
hands on him?

DOGBERRY   Truly, by your office you may, but I think
they that touch pitch will be defiled. The most peace-   56
able way for you, if you do take a thief, is to let him
show himself what he is and steal out of your company.

VERGES   You have been always called a merciful man,
partner.

DOGBERRY   Truly, I would not hang a dog by my will,
much more a man who hath any honesty in him.

VERGES   If you hear a child cry in the night, you must
call to the nurse and bid her still it.

WATCH   How if the nurse be asleep and will not hear
us?

DOGBERRY   Why then depart in peace, and let the child
wake her with crying, for the ewe that will not hear
her lamb when it baas will never answer a calf when
he bleats.

VERGES   'Tis very true.

DOGBERRY   This is the end of the charge: you, Constable,
are to present the Prince's own person. If you meet the   74
Prince in the night, you may stay him.

VERGES   Nay, by 'r Lady, that I think 'a cannot.   76

DOGBERRY   Five shillings to one on 't, with any man that
knows the statutes, he may stay him; marry, not without the Prince be willing, for indeed the watch ought
to offend no man, and it is an offense to stay a man
against his will.

VERGES   By 'r Lady, I think it be so.

DOGBERRY   Ha, ah ha! Well, masters, good night. An

---

50 true honest   **51 meddle or make** have to do   **52 is** it is   **56 they . . .
defiled** (A commonplace derived from Ecclesiasticus 13:1.)   **74 present**
represent   **76 by 'r Lady** i.e., by Our Lady. (A mild oath.)

there be any matter of weight chances, call up me.
Keep your fellows' counsels and your own, and good
night. Come, neighbor. [*He starts to leave with Verges.*]

SEACOAL Well, masters, we hear our charge. Let us go
sit here upon the church bench till two, and then all
to bed.

DOGBERRY One word more, honest neighbors. I pray
you, watch about Signor Leonato's door, for the wedding being there tomorrow, there is a great coil to- 92
night. Adieu. Be vigitant, I beseech you. 93

                Exeunt [Dogberry and Verges].

   Enter Borachio and Conrade.

BORACHIO What, Conrade!

SEACOAL [*Aside*] Peace! Stir not.

BORACHIO Conrade, I say!

CONRADE Here, man. I am at thy elbow.

BORACHIO Mass, and my elbow itched; I thought there 98
would a scab follow. 99

CONRADE I will owe thee an answer for that; and now 100
forward with thy tale.

BORACHIO Stand thee close, then, under this pent- 102
house, for it drizzles rain, and I will, like a true drunk- 103
ard, utter all to thee. 104

SEACOAL [*Aside*] Some treason, masters. Yet stand 105
close. 106

BORACHIO Therefore know I have earned of Don John a
thousand ducats.

CONRADE Is it possible that any villainy should be so
dear? 110

BORACHIO Thou shouldst rather ask if it were possible
any villainy should be so rich; for when rich villains 112
have need of poor ones, poor ones may make what
price they will.

---

92 coil to-do   **93 vigitant** (For *vigilant.*)   **98 Mass** i.e., by the Mass.   **my
elbow itched** (Proverbially a warning against questionable compan-
ions.)   **99 scab** i.e., scoundrel (with play on literal meaning)   **100 owe
thee an answer** answer later   **102–103 penthouse** overhanging structure   **103–104 true drunkard** (Alludes to the commonplace that the
drunkard tells all; Borachio's name in Spanish means "drunkard.")
105–106 stand close stay hidden   **110 dear** expensive   **112 villainy** i.e.,
instigator of villainy

CONRADE   I wonder at it.

BORACHIO   That shows thou art unconfirmed. Thou 116
knowest that the fashion of a doublet, or a hat, or a
cloak, is nothing to a man. 118

CONRADE   Yes, it is apparel.

BORACHIO   I mean, the fashion.

CONRADE   Yes, the fashion is the fashion.

BORACHIO   Tush, I may as well say the fool's the fool.
But seest thou not what a deformed thief this fashion 123
is?

SEACOAL [Aside]   I know that Deformed. 'A has been a
vile thief this seven year; 'a goes up and down like a 126
gentleman. I remember his name.

BORACHIO   Didst thou not hear somebody?

CONRADE   No, 'twas the vane on the house.

BORACHIO   Seest thou not, I say, what a deformed thief
this fashion is, how giddily 'a turns about all the hot
bloods between fourteen and five-and-thirty, sometimes fashioning them like Pharaoh's soldiers in the
reechy painting, sometimes like god Bel's priests in the 134
old church-window, sometimes like the shaven Her- 135
cules in the smirched worm-eaten tapestry, where his 136
codpiece seems as massy as his club? 137

CONRADE   All this I see, and I see that the fashion wears 138
out more apparel than the man. But art not thou thy- 139
self giddy with the fashion too, that thou hast shifted
out of thy tale into telling me of the fashion?

BORACHIO   Not so, neither. But know that I have tonight
wooed Margaret, the Lady Hero's gentlewoman, by

---

116 unconfirmed inexperienced   **118 is . . . man** does not make the man.
(But Conrade plays on the phrase in its usual sense.)   **123 deformed thief**
i.e., so called because fashion takes such varied and extreme shapes and
because it impoverishes those who follow fashion   **126 up and down**
about, here and there   **134 reechy** dirty, grimy. (Perhaps this painting is of
the Israelites passing through the Red Sea.)   **god Bel's priests** (Probably
alludes to the story of Bel and the Dragon, from the apocryphal Book of
Daniel, depicted in a stained-glass window.)   **135–136 shaven Hercules** (A
reference either to Hercules in the service of Omphale—see 2.1.242, note—
or, confusedly, to the story of Samson.)   **137 codpiece** decorative pouch at
the front of a man's breeches (indelicately conspicuous in this tapestry)
138–139 fashion . . . man i.e., fashion prompts the discarding of clothes
faster than honest use

the name of Hero. She leans me out at her mistress' 144
chamber window, bids me a thousand times good
night—I tell this tale vilely; I should first tell thee how
the Prince, Claudio, and my master, planted and
placed and possessed by my master Don John, saw afar 148
off in the orchard this amiable encounter. 149

CONRADE   And thought they Margaret was Hero?

BORACHIO   Two of them did, the Prince and Claudio,
but the devil my master knew she was Margaret; and
partly by his oaths, which first possessed them, partly
by the dark night, which did deceive them, but chiefly
by my villainy, which did confirm any slander that
Don John had made, away went Claudio enraged;
swore he would meet her, as he was appointed, next
morning at the temple, and there, before the whole
congregation, shame her with what he saw o'ernight
and send her home again without a husband.

SEACOAL   We charge you, in the Prince's name, stand!

FIRST WATCH   Call up the right Master Constable. We 162
have here recovered the most dangerous piece of lech- 163
ery that ever was known in the commonwealth. 164

SEACOAL   And one Deformed is one of them. I know
him; 'a wears a lock. 166

CONRADE   Masters, masters—

FIRST WATCH   You'll be made bring Deformed forth, I
warrant you.

CONRADE   Masters—

SEACOAL   Never speak, we charge you. Let us obey you 171
to go with us. 172

BORACHIO   We are like to prove a goodly commodity, 173
being taken up of these men's bills. 174

CONRADE   A commodity in question, I warrant you. 175
Come, we'll obey you.   *Exeunt.*

❖

144 leans me leans. (*Me* is an emphatic marker.)   **148 possessed** (mis-
leadingly) informed; also, perhaps, possessed as by the devil
149 amiable amorous   **162 right Master Constable** (A comic title on the
pattern of "Right Worshipful," etc.)   **163 recovered** (For *discovered*.)
163-164 lechery (For *treachery*.)   **166 lock** lock of hair hanging down on
the left shoulder; the lovelock   **171-172 Let . . . to** (A blunder for *obey
us and*.)   **173 commodity** goods acquired   **174 taken up** (1) arrested
(2) obtained on credit.   **bills** (1) pikes (2) bonds given as security   **175 in
question** (1) subject to judicial examination (2) of doubtful value

3.4   *Enter Hero, and Margaret and Ursula.*

HERO   Good Ursula, wake my cousin Beatrice and desire her to rise.

URSULA   I will, lady.

HERO   And bid her come hither.

URSULA   Well.   *[Exit.]* 5

MARGARET   Troth, I think your other rabato were better. 6

HERO   No, pray thee, good Meg, I'll wear this.

MARGARET   By my troth, 's not so good, and I warrant 8
your cousin will say so.

HERO   My cousin's a fool, and thou art another. I'll wear
none but this.

MARGARET   I like the new tire within excellently, if the 12
hair were a thought browner; and your gown's a most 13
rare fashion, i' faith. I saw the Duchess of Milan's
gown that they praise so.

HERO   O, that exceeds, they say.   16

MARGARET   By my troth, 's but a nightgown in respect 17
of yours: cloth o' gold, and cuts, and laced with silver, 18
set with pearls, down sleeves, side sleeves, and skirts, 19
round underborne with a bluish tinsel. But for a fine, 20
quaint, graceful, and excellent fashion, yours is worth 21
ten on 't.

HERO   God give me joy to wear it! For my heart is exceeding heavy.

MARGARET   'Twill be heavier soon by the weight of
a man.

HERO   Fie upon thee! Art not ashamed?

MARGARET   Of what, lady? Of speaking honorably? Is
not marriage honorable in a beggar? Is not your lord 29

3.4. Location: Leonato's house.
5 Well very well, as you wish   **6 rabato** tall collar supporting a ruff,
stiffened with wire or starch   **8 troth, 's** faith, it is   **12 tire within**
headdress in the inner room   **13 hair** hairpiece attached to the *tire*
(l. 12)   **16 exceeds** i.e., exceeds comparison   **17 nightgown** dressing
gown   **17–18 in respect of** compared to   **18 cuts** slashes in a garment
revealing the underlying fabric.   **laced** trimmed.   **silver** i.e., silver
thread   **19 down sleeves** tight-fitting sleeves to the wrist.   **side sleeves**
secondary ornamental sleeves hanging from the shoulder   **20 round
underborne** with a lining around the edge of the skirt.   **tinsel** cloth,
usually silk, interwoven with threads of silver or gold   **21 quaint** elegant   **29 in** even in

honorable without marriage? I think you would have
me say, "saving your reverence, a husband." An bad   31
thinking do not wrest true speaking, I'll offend no-   32
body. Is there any harm in "the heavier for a husband"? None, I think, an it be the right husband and
the right wife; otherwise 'tis light, and not heavy. Ask 35
my Lady Beatrice else. Here she comes.

Enter Beatrice.

HERO   Good morrow, coz.
BEATRICE   Good morrow, sweet Hero.
HERO   Why, how now? Do you speak in the sick tune?   39
BEATRICE   I am out of all other tune, methinks.
MARGARET   Clap 's into "Light o' love." That goes with- 41
out a burden; do you sing it, and I'll dance it.   42
BEATRICE   Ye light o' love with your heels! Then, if your 43
husband have stables enough, you'll see he shall lack
no barns.   45
MARGARET   O illegitimate construction! I scorn that with 46
my heels.   47
BEATRICE   'Tis almost five o'clock, cousin; 'tis time you
were ready. By my troth, I am exceeding ill. Heigh-ho!
MARGARET   For a hawk, a horse, or a husband?
BEATRICE   For the letter that begins them all, H.   51
MARGARET   Well, an you be not turned Turk, there's no 52
more sailing by the star.   53
BEATRICE   What means the fool, trow?   54
MARGARET   Nothing I; but God send everyone their
heart's desire!

---

31 **saving . . . husband** (By this apologetic formula, Margaret suggests
that Hero is too prudish even to hear the word *husband* mentioned.)
An bad if bawdy   32 **wrest** misinterpret   35 **light** (with a play on the
meaning "wanton")   39 **tune** i.e., mood   41 **Clap 's** let's shift.   **Light o'
love** (A popular song.)   42 **burden** bass accompaniment (with play on
the idea of "a weight of a man")   43 **Ye . . . heels** i.e., you're light-
heeled, wanton   45 **barns** (with pun on *bairns*, children)   46–47 **with
my heels** (A proverbial expression of scorn.)   51 **H** (with a pun on *ache*,
pronounced "aitch")   52 **turned Turk** i.e., turned apostate to the true
faith (by violating your oath not to become a lover)   52–53 **no . . . star**
no more navigating by the North Star, i.e., no certain truth in which to
trust   54 **trow** I wonder

HERO   These gloves the Count sent me, they are an excellent perfume.   58

BEATRICE   I am stuffed, cousin; I cannot smell.   59

MARGARET   A maid, and stuffed! There's goodly catch-
ing of cold.

BEATRICE   O, God help me, God help me! How long
have you professed apprehension?   63

MARGARET   Ever since you left it. Doth not my wit become me rarely?

BEATRICE   It is not seen enough; you should wear it in   66
your cap. By my troth, I am sick.   67

MARGARET   Get you some of this distilled *carduus bene-*   68
dictus and lay it to your heart. It is the only thing for 69
a qualm.

HERO   There thou prick'st her with a thistle.

BEATRICE   *Benedictus!* Why *benedictus*? You have some
moral in this *benedictus*.   73

MARGARET   Moral? No, by my troth, I have no moral
meaning, I meant plain holy-thistle. You may think
perchance that I think you are in love. Nay, by 'r Lady,
I am not such a fool to think what I list, nor I list not to
think what I can, nor indeed I cannot think, if I would
think my heart out of thinking, that you are in love or
that you will be in love or that you can be in love. Yet
Benedick was such another, and now is he become a   81
man. He swore he would never marry, and yet now,   82
in despite of his heart, he eats his meat without grudg-   83
ing; and how you may be converted I know not, but   84
methinks you look with your eyes as other women do.

BEATRICE   What pace is this that thy tongue keeps?

MARGARET   Not a false gallop.   87

    Enter Ursula.

58 perfume (Gloves were often perfumed.)   **59 stuffed** i.e., stuffed up
with a cold. (But Margaret takes it in a bawdy sense.)   **63 professed**
apprehension made claim to be witty   **66–67 wear . . . cap** i.e., as a fool
does his coxcomb   **68–69 carduus benedictus** the blessed thistle, noted
for medicinal properties (with a pun on *Benedick*)   **73 moral** hidden
meaning   **81–82 a man** i.e., like other men   **83–84 eats . . . grudging**
i.e., is content to be like other men, to be in love   **87 Not . . . gallop** not
a forced burst of speed (i.e., I speak the truth)

URSULA   Madam, withdraw. The Prince, the Count, Signor Benedick, Don John, and all the gallants of the
town are come to fetch you to church.

HERO   Help to dress me, good coz, good Meg, good Ursula.   [*Exeunt.*]

❧

3.5   *Enter Leonato and the Constable [Dogberry]
and the Headborough [Verges].*

LEONATO   What would you with me, honest neighbor?

DOGBERRY   Marry, sir, I would have some confidence   2
with you that decerns you nearly.   3

LEONATO   Brief, I pray you, for you see it is a busy time
with me.

DOGBERRY   Marry, this it is, sir.

VERGES   Yes, in truth it is, sir.

LEONATO   What is it, my good friends?

DOGBERRY   Goodman Verges, sir, speaks a little off the   9
matter—an old man, sir, and his wits are not so blunt   10
as, God help, I would desire they were, but, in faith,
honest as the skin between his brows.   12

VERGES   Yes, I thank God I am as honest as any man
living that is an old man and no honester than I.

DOGBERRY   Comparisons are odorous. *Palabras*, neigh-   15
bor Verges.

LEONATO   Neighbors, you are tedious.

DOGBERRY   It pleases your worship to say so, but we are
the poor Duke's officers; but truly, for mine own part,   19
if I were as tedious as a king, I could find in my heart
to bestow it all of your worship.   21

LEONATO   All thy tediousness on me, ah?

DOGBERRY   Yea, an 'twere a thousand pound more than

3.5. Location: Leonato's house.
s.d. Headborough local constable   **2 confidence** (A blunder for *conference*.)   **3 decerns** (For *concerns*.)   **9 Goodman** (Title of persons under
the social rank of gentleman.)   **10 blunt** (He means *sharp*.)   **12 honest
. . . brows** (Proverbial expression of honesty.)   **15 odorous** (For *odi-
ous*.)   **Palabras** (For *pocas palabras*, "few words" in Spanish.)   **19 poor
Duke's officers** (For *Duke's poor officers*.)   **21 of on**

'tis; for I hear as good exclamation on your worship as 24
of any man in the city, and though I be but a poor
man, I am glad to hear it.

VERGES   And so am I.

LEONATO   I would fain know what you have to say.

VERGES   Marry, sir, our watch tonight, excepting your 29
worship's presence, ha' ta'en a couple of as arrant 30
knaves as any in Messina.

DOGBERRY   A good old man, sir; he will be talking. As
they say, "When the age is in, the wit is out." God 33
help us, it is a world to see! Well said, i' faith, neigh- 34
bor Verges. Well, God's a good man. An two men 35
ride of a horse, one must ride behind. An honest soul, 36
i' faith, sir, by my troth he is, as ever broke bread, but
God is to be worshiped, all men are not alike, alas,
good neighbor!

LEONATO   Indeed, neighbor, he comes too short of you.

DOGBERRY   Gifts that God gives.

LEONATO   I must leave you.

DOGBERRY   One word, sir. Our watch, sir, have indeed
comprehended two aspicious persons, and we would 44
have them this morning examined before your worship.

LEONATO   Take their examination yourself and bring
it me. I am now in great haste, as it may appear
unto you.

DOGBERRY   It shall be suffigance.   50

LEONATO   Drink some wine ere you go. Fare you well.

     [*Enter a Messenger.*]

MESSENGER   My lord, they stay for you to give your
daughter to her husband.

LEONATO   I'll wait upon them. I am ready.   54
                    [*Exeunt Leonato and Messenger.*]

---

24 exclamation (Possibly for *acclamation*.)   **29 tonight** last night.   **except-**
ing (For *respecting*.)   **30 ha'** have   **33 When . . . out** (An adaptation of the
proverb, "When ale is in, wit is out.")   **34 a world** i.e., wonderful. (Proverbial.)   **35 God 's . . . man** i.e., God is good. (A proverbial saying.)   **36 of**
on   **44 comprehended** (For *apprehended*.)   **aspicious** (For *suspicious*.)
50 suffigance (For *sufficient*.)   **54 wait upon** attend

DOGBERRY   Go, good partner, go, get you to Francis Sea- 55
  coal. Bid him bring his pen and inkhorn to the jail. We 56
  are now to examination these men. 57
VERGES   And we must do it wisely.
DOGBERRY   We will spare for no wit, I warrant you.
  Here's that shall drive some of them to a noncome. 60
  Only get the learned writer to set down our excom- 61
  munication, and meet me at the jail.   [*Exeunt.*] 62

❖

55–56 Francis Seacoal i.e., the Sexton of 4.2, not the member of the
watch in 3.3   **57 examination** (For *examine.*)   **60 noncome** (Probably a
contraction for *non compos mentis,* "not of sound mind," but Dogberry
may have intended *nonplus.*)   **61–62 excommunication** (For *examination*
or *communication.*)

4.1 *Enter Prince [Don Pedro], [Don John the]*
Bastard, Leonato, Friar [Francis], Claudio,
Benedick, Hero, and Beatrice [with attendants].

LEONATO Come, Friar Francis, be brief—only to the
plain form of marriage, and you shall recount their
particular duties afterwards.

FRIAR You come hither, my lord, to marry this lady?

CLAUDIO No.

LEONATO To be married to her. Friar, you come to
marry her.

FRIAR Lady, you come hither to be married to this
Count?

HERO I do.

FRIAR If either of you know any inward impediment 11
why you should not be conjoined, I charge you on
your souls to utter it.

CLAUDIO Know you any, Hero?

HERO None, my lord.

FRIAR Know you any, Count?

LEONATO I dare make his answer, none.

CLAUDIO O, what men dare do! What men may do!
What men daily do, not knowing what they do!

BENEDICK How now? Interjections? Why, then, some 20
be of laughing, as ah, ha, he! 21

CLAUDIO
Stand thee by, Friar. Father, by your leave, 22
Will you with free and unconstrainèd soul
Give me this maid, your daughter?

LEONATO
As freely, son, as God did give her me.

CLAUDIO
And what have I to give you back, whose worth
May counterpoise this rich and precious gift? 27

DON PEDRO
Nothing, unless you render her again.

4.1. Location: A church.
11 inward secret **20–21 some . . . he** (Benedick quotes from Lilly's
Latin grammar on the subject of interjections; according to Lilly, these
are to be classified as laughing interjections.) **22 Stand thee by** stand
aside **27 counterpoise** balance, be equivalent to

CLAUDIO
Sweet Prince, you learn me noble thankfulness.   29
                    [*He hands Hero to Leonato.*]
There, Leonato, take her back again.
Give not this rotten orange to your friend;
She's but the sign and semblance of her honor.   32
Behold how like a maid she blushes here!
O, what authority and show of truth   34
Can cunning sin cover itself withal!
Comes not that blood as modest evidence   36
To witness simple virtue? Would you not swear,   37
All you that see her, that she were a maid,
By these exterior shows? But she is none:
She knows the heat of a luxurious bed.   40
Her blush is guiltiness, not modesty.

LEONATO
What do you mean, my lord?

CLAUDIO   Not to be married,
Not to knit my soul to an approvèd wanton.   43

LEONATO
Dear my lord, if you, in your own proof,   44
Have vanquished the resistance of her youth,
And made defeat of her virginity—

CLAUDIO
I know what you would say: if I have known her,
You will say she did embrace me as a husband,
And so extenuate the forehand sin.   49
No, Leonato,
I never tempted her with word too large,   51
But, as a brother to his sister, showed
Bashful sincerity and comely love.

HERO
And seemed I ever otherwise to you?

CLAUDIO
Out on thee, seeming! I will write against it.   55

29 learn teach   **32 sign and semblance** pretense and outward show
34 authority assurance   **36 blood** i.e., blush.   **modest evidence** evidence
of modesty   **37 witness** bear witness to   **40 luxurious** lascivious,
lustful   **43 approvèd** proved   **44 in . . . proof** in making trial of her
yourself   **49 extenuate** excuse, lessen.   **forehand sin** sin of anticipating
(marriage)   **51 large** broad, immodest   **55 Out . . . seeming** i.e., shame
on you, a mere semblance of good

You seem to me as Dian in her orb,   56
As chaste as is the bud ere it be blown;   57
But you are more intemperate in your blood
Than Venus, or those pampered animals
That rage in savage sensuality.

HERO
  Is my lord well, that he doth speak so wide?   61

LEONATO
  Sweet Prince, why speak not you?

DON PEDRO   What should I speak?
  I stand dishonored, that have gone about   63
  To link my dear friend to a common stale.   64

LEONATO
  Are these things spoken, or do I but dream?

DON JOHN
  Sir, they are spoken, and these things are true.

BENEDICK   This looks not like a nuptial.

HERO   True! O God!   68

CLAUDIO   Leonato, stand I here?
  Is this the Prince? Is this the Prince's brother?
  Is this face Hero's? Are our eyes our own?

LEONATO
  All this is so. But what of this, my lord?

CLAUDIO
  Let me but move one question to your daughter,
  And by that fatherly and kindly power   74
  That you have in her, bid her answer truly.

LEONATO
  I charge thee do so, as thou art my child.

HERO
  O, God defend me, how am I beset!
  What kind of catechizing call you this?   78

CLAUDIO
  To make you answer truly to your name.

HERO
  Is it not Hero? Who can blot that name
  With any just reproach?

---

56 Dian . . . orb i.e., Diana, goddess of chastity, enthroned in the moon
57 be blown open, flower   **61 wide** wide of the mark   **63 gone about**
undertaken   **64 stale** whore   **68 True** (A reply to Don John's speech.)
74 kindly natural   **78 catechizing** formal questioning used by the
Church to teach the principles of faith

CLAUDIO   Marry, that can Hero!
Hero itself can blot out Hero's virtue.   82
What man was he talked with you yesternight
Out at your window betwixt twelve and one?
Now, if you are a maid, answer to this.

HERO
I talked with no man at that hour, my lord.

DON PEDRO
Why, then are you no maiden. Leonato,
I am sorry you must hear. Upon mine honor,
Myself, my brother, and this grievèd Count   89
Did see her, hear her, at that hour last night
Talk with a ruffian at her chamber window,
Who hath indeed, most like a liberal villain,   92
Confessed the vile encounters they have had
A thousand times in secret.

DON JOHN
Fie, fie, they are not to be named, my lord,
Not to be spoke of!
There is not chastity enough in language
Without offense to utter them. Thus, pretty lady,
I am sorry for thy much misgovernment.   99

CLAUDIO
O Hero, what a Hero hadst thou been,
If half thy outward graces had been placed
About thy thoughts and counsels of thy heart!
But fare thee well, most foul, most fair! Farewell,
Thou pure impiety and impious purity!
For thee I'll lock up all the gates of love,   105
And on my eyelids shall conjecture hang,   106
To turn all beauty into thoughts of harm,
And never shall it more be gracious.   108

LEONATO
Hath no man's dagger here a point for me?
                              [Hero swoons.]

82 Hero itself the name Hero (which in the story of Hero and Leander
became a name for a faithful lover)   89 grievèd (1) aggrieved, wronged
(2) struck with grief   92 liberal licentious   99 much misgovernment
great misconduct   105 For thee because of you   106 conjecture evil
suspicion   108 be gracious seem attractive, graceful

BEATRICE
Why, how now, cousin, wherefore sink you down?
DON JOHN
Come, let us go. These things, come thus to light,
Smother her spirits up.
          [*Exeunt Don Pedro, Don John, and Claudio.*]
BENEDICK
How doth the lady?
BEATRICE   Dead, I think. Help, uncle!
Hero, why, Hero! Uncle! Signor Benedick! Friar!
LEONATO
O Fate, take not away thy heavy hand!
Death is the fairest cover for her shame
That may be wished for.
BEATRICE   How now, cousin Hero?
FRIAR Have comfort, lady.
LEONATO
Dost thou look up?
FRIAR   Yea, wherefore should she not?   119
LEONATO
Wherefore? Why, doth not every earthly thing
Cry shame upon her? Could she here deny
The story that is printed in her blood?   122
Do not live, Hero, do not ope thine eyes;   123
For, did I think thou wouldst not quickly die,
Thought I thy spirits were stronger than thy shames,   125
Myself would, on the rearward of reproaches,   126
Strike at thy life. Grieved I, I had but one?
Chid I for that at frugal nature's frame?   128
O, one too much by thee! Why had I one?
Why ever wast thou lovely in my eyes?
Why had I not with charitable hand
Took up a beggar's issue at my gates,
Who, smirchèd thus and mired with infamy,   133
I might have said, "No part of it is mine;
This shame derives itself from unknown loins"?

---

119 wherefore why **122 blood** i.e., blushes **123 ope** open **125 spirits**
life-giving energies, vital powers **126 on . . . reproaches** following this
public disgrace **128 Chid** chided. **frame** plan, order **133 smirchèd**
defamed. **mired** defiled

But mine, and mine I loved, and mine I praised,
And mine that I was proud on, mine so much
That I myself was to myself not mine,   138
Valuing of her—why, she, O she, is fallen   139
Into a pit of ink, that the wide sea
Hath drops too few to wash her clean again
And salt too little which may season give   142
To her foul-tainted flesh!
BENEDICK   Sir, sir, be patient.
For my part, I am so attired in wonder,   144
I know not what to say.
BEATRICE
O, on my soul, my cousin is belied!
BENEDICK
Lady, were you her bedfellow last night?
BEATRICE
No, truly, not; although, until last night,
I have this twelvemonth been her bedfellow.
LEONATO
Confirmed, confirmed! O, that is stronger made
Which was before barred up with ribs of iron!   151
Would the two princes lie and Claudio lie,
Who loved her so that, speaking of her foulness,
Washed it with tears? Hence from her! Let her die.
FRIAR   Hear me a little;
For I have only been silent so long
And given way unto this course of fortune   157
By noting of the lady. I have marked   158
A thousand blushing apparitions
To start into her face, a thousand innocent shames
In angel whiteness beat away those blushes,
And in her eye there hath appeared a fire
To burn the errors that these princes hold   163
Against her maiden truth. Call me a fool;
Trust not my reading nor my observations,

138–139 That . . . her i.e., that I set no value on myself in caring so
much for her   **142 season** preservative   **144 attired in wonder** i.e., filled
with amazement   **151 before** already   **157 given way unto** i.e., accepted.   **course of fortune** turn of events   **158 By . . . lady** i.e., so that I
might observe, or because I have been observing, Hero's reaction (?)
163 errors (Personified as a heretic burned at the stake.)

Which with experimental seal doth warrant   166
The tenor of my book; trust not my age,   167
My reverence, calling, nor divinity,
If this sweet lady lie not guiltless here
Under some biting error.

LEONATO   Friar, it cannot be.
Thou seest that all the grace that she hath left
Is that she will not add to her damnation
A sin of perjury; she not denies it.
Why seek'st thou then to cover with excuse
That which appears in proper nakedness?   175

FRIAR
Lady, what man is he you are accused of?

HERO
They know that do accuse me; I know none.
If I know more of any man alive
Than that which maiden modesty doth warrant,   179
Let all my sins lack mercy! O my father,
Prove you that any man with me conversed   181
At hours unmeet or that I yesternight   182
Maintained the change of words with any creature,   183
Refuse me, hate me, torture me to death!   184

FRIAR
There is some strange misprision in the princes.   185

BENEDICK
Two of them have the very bent of honor;   186
And if their wisdoms be misled in this,
The practice of it lives in John the Bastard,   188
Whose spirits toil in frame of villainies.   189

LEONATO
I know not. If they speak but truth of her,
These hands shall tear her; if they wrong her honor,
The proudest of them shall well hear of it.
Time hath not yet so dried this blood of mine,

166–167 Which . . . book i.e., by means of which observations and
experience I have confirmed what I learned from books   175 proper its
own   179 warrant sanction, permit   181 Prove you if you prove
182 unmeet improper   183 Maintained the change held exchange
184 Refuse disown   185 misprision mistake, misunderstanding
186 the very bent of an absolute inclination of the mind toward
188 practice scheming   189 frame contriving

Nor age so eat up my invention,   194
Nor fortune made such havoc of my means,
Nor my bad life reft me so much of friends,   196
But they shall find, awaked in such a kind,   197
Both strength of limb and policy of mind,   198
Ability in means, and choice of friends,
To quit me of them throughly.
FRIAR   Pause awhile,   200
And let my counsel sway you in this case.
Your daughter here the princes left for dead.
Let her awhile be secretly kept in,
And publish it that she is dead indeed;
Maintain a mourning ostentation,   205
And on your family's old monument   206
Hang mournful epitaphs, and do all rites
That appertain unto a burial.
LEONATO
What shall become of this? What will this do?   209
FRIAR
Marry, this well carried shall on her behalf   210
Change slander to remorse. That is some good.
But not for that dream I on this strange course,   212
But on this travail look for greater birth.   213
She dying, as it must be so maintained,
Upon the instant that she was accused,
Shall be lamented, pitied, and excused
Of every hearer; for it so falls out
That what we have we prize not to the worth   218
Whiles we enjoy it, but being lacked and lost,
Why then we rack the value, then we find   220
The virtue that possession would not show us
Whiles it was ours. So will it fare with Claudio.
When he shall hear she died upon his words,   223
Th' idea of her life shall sweetly creep

194 eat eaten. (Pronounced "et.") invention power to plan (vengeance) 196 reft robbed 197 kind manner 198 policy shrewdness,
contriving 200 quit . . . throughly revenge myself on them thor-
oughly · 205 Maintain . . . ostentation perform all the outward signs of
mourning 206 monument burial vault 209 become of result from
210 carried managed 212 that i.e., to "change slander to remorse"
213 on this travail (1) as a result of this effort (2) from this labor in
childbirth 218 to the worth as fully as it deserves 220 rack stretch
(as on a rack) 223 upon in consequence of

Into his study of imagination,   225
And every lovely organ of her life   226
Shall come appareled in more precious habit,   227
More moving, delicate, and full of life,
Into the eye and prospect of his soul,   229
Than when she lived indeed. Then shall he mourn,
If ever love had interest in his liver,   231
And wish he had not so accusèd her,
No, though he thought his accusation true.
Let this be so, and doubt not but success   234
Will fashion the event in better shape   235
Than I can lay it down in likelihood.   236
But if all aim but this be leveled false,   237
The supposition of the lady's death
Will quench the wonder of her infamy.
And if it sort not well, you may conceal her,   240
As best befits her wounded reputation,
In some reclusive and religious life,   242
Out of all eyes, tongues, minds, and injuries.   243

BENEDICK
Signor Leonato, let the Friar advise you;
And though you know my inwardness and love   245
Is very much unto the Prince and Claudio,
Yet, by mine honor, I will deal in this
As secretly and justly as your soul
Should with your body.

LEONATO   Being that I flow in grief, 249
The smallest twine may lead me.

FRIAR
'Tis well consented. Presently away;   251
    For to strange sores strangely they strain the cure.   252
Come, lady, die to live. This wedding day

---

225 **study of imagination** musing, imaginative contemplation
226 **organ . . . life** aspect of her when she was alive   227 **habit** apparel   229 **prospect** range of vision   231 **interest in** claim upon.   **liver** (The supposed seat of the passion of love.)   234 **success** i.e., what succeeds or happens in time as my plan unfolds   235 **event** outcome
236 **lay . . . likelihood** anticipate its probable course   237 **if . . . false** i.e., if every other aim miscarry   240 **sort** turn out   242 **reclusive** cloistered   243 **injuries** insults   245 **inwardness and love** close friendship   249 **Being that** seeing that, since.   **flow in** overflow with, or am afloat in   251 **Presently** immediately   252 **For . . . cure** strange diseases require strange and desperate cures

Perhaps is but prolonged. Have patience and endure.   254
    Exit [with all but Benedick and Beatrice].

BENEDICK   Lady Beatrice, have you wept all this while?

BEATRICE   Yea, and I will weep a while longer.

BENEDICK   I will not desire that.

BEATRICE   You have no reason; I do it freely.

BENEDICK   Surely I do believe your fair cousin is wronged.

BEATRICE   Ah, how much might the man deserve of me that would right her!

BENEDICK   Is there any way to show such friendship?

BEATRICE   A very even way, but no such friend.   264

BENEDICK   May a man do it?

BEATRICE   It is a man's office, but not yours.   266

BENEDICK   I do love nothing in the world so well as you. Is not that strange?

BEATRICE   As strange as the thing I know not. It were as possible for me to say I loved nothing so well as you. But believe me not; and yet I lie not. I confess nothing, nor I deny nothing. I am sorry for my cousin.

BENEDICK   By my sword, Beatrice, thou lovest me.

BEATRICE   Do not swear and eat it.   274

BENEDICK   I will swear by it that you love me, and I will make him eat it that says I love not you.

BEATRICE   Will you not eat your word?

BENEDICK   With no sauce that can be devised to it. I pro-   278
test I love thee.   279

BEATRICE   Why, then, God forgive me!

BENEDICK   What offense, sweet Beatrice?

BEATRICE   You have stayed me in a happy hour. I was   282
about to protest I loved you.

BENEDICK   And do it with all thy heart.

BEATRICE   I love you with so much of my heart that none is left to protest.

BENEDICK   Come, bid me do anything for thee.

BEATRICE   Kill Claudio.

BENEDICK   Ha! Not for the wide world.

BEATRICE   You kill me to deny it. Farewell.   *[Going.]*   290

---

254 prolonged deferred, put off   **264 even** direct, straightforward
266 office duty   **274 eat it** i.e., eat your words   **278–279 protest** af-
firm   **282 stayed** stopped.   **in . . . hour** at an appropriate moment
290 it i.e., my request

BENEDICK   Tarry, sweet Beatrice.

BEATRICE   I am gone, though I am here. There is no love 292
in you. Nay, I pray you, let me go.

BENEDICK   Beatrice—

BEATRICE   In faith, I will go.

BENEDICK   We'll be friends first.

BEATRICE   You dare easier be friends with me than fight
with mine enemy.

BENEDICK   Is Claudio thine enemy?

BEATRICE   Is 'a not approved in the height a villain, that 300
hath slandered, scorned, dishonored my kinswoman?
O, that I were a man! What, bear her in hand until they 302
come to take hands, and then, with public accusation,
uncovered slander, unmitigated rancor—O God, that 304
I were a man! I would eat his heart in the market-
place.

BENEDICK   Hear me, Beatrice—

BEATRICE   Talk with a man out at a window! A proper
saying!

BENEDICK   Nay, but Beatrice—

BEATRICE   Sweet Hero! She is wronged, she is slandered,
she is undone.

BENEDICK   Beat—

BEATRICE   Princes and counties! Surely, a princely testi- 314
mony, a goodly count, Count Comfect; a sweet gallant, 315
surely! O, that I were a man for his sake! Or that I had
any friend would be a man for my sake! But manhood
is melted into curtsies, valor into compliment, and
men are only turned into tongue, and trim ones too. 319
He is now as valiant as Hercules that only tells a lie 320
and swears it. I cannot be a man with wishing, therefore I will die a woman with grieving.

BENEDICK   Tarry, good Beatrice. By this hand, I love
thee.

BEATRICE   Use it for my love some other way than
swearing by it.

---

292 gone i.e., in spirit   **300 approved** proved.   **height** extreme
302 bear her in hand delude her with false hopes   **304 uncovered**
open, unconcealed   **314 counties** counts   **315 count** (1) the title
(2) declaration of complaint in an indictment.   **Comfect** candy or
sweetmeat   **319 trim** nice, elegant, fine. (Used ironically.)   **320 now**
nowadays considered

BENEDICK Think you in your soul the Count Claudio
hath wronged Hero?

BEATRICE Yea, as sure as I have a thought or a soul.

BENEDICK Enough, I am engaged. I will challenge him. 330
I will kiss your hand, and so I leave you. By this hand,
Claudio shall render me a dear account. As you hear 332
of me, so think of me. Go, comfort your cousin. I must
say she is dead; and so, farewell. [*Exeunt separately.*]

✤

4.2 *Enter the Constables [Dogberry and Verges]*
and the Town Clerk [Sexton] in gowns,
Borachio, [Conrade, and Watch].

DOGBERRY Is our whole dissembly appeared?   1

VERGES O, a stool and a cushion for the sexton.
  [*Stool and cushion are brought. The Sexton sits.*]

SEXTON Which be the malefactors?

DOGBERRY Marry, that am I and my partner.

VERGES Nay, that's certain, we have the exhibition to 5
examine.

SEXTON But which are the offenders that are to be examined? Let them come before Master Constable.

DOGBERRY Yea, marry, let them come before me. [*The
prisoners are brought forward.*] What is your name,
friend?

BORACHIO Borachio.

DOGBERRY Pray, write down Borachio. Yours, sirrah? 13

CONRADE I am a gentleman, sir, and my name is Conrade.

DOGBERRY Write down Master Gentleman Conrade.
Masters, do you serve God?

CONRADE, BORACHIO Yea, sir, we hope.

DOGBERRY Write down that they hope they serve God;
and write God first, for God defend but God should 20
go before such villains! Masters, it is proved already

330 **I am engaged** I pledge myself   332 **dear** costly

4.2. Location: The jail.
1 **dissembly** (A blunder for *assembly*.)   5 **exhibition** (Possibly for *com-*
mission.)   13 **sirrah** (Used to address inferiors; Conrade objects.)
20 **defend** forbid

that you are little better than false knaves, and it will
go near to be thought so shortly. How answer you for
yourselves?

CONRADE Marry, sir, we say we are none.

DOGBERRY A marvelous witty fellow, I assure you, but 26
I will go about with him. [*To Borachio.*] Come you 27
hither, sirrah, a word in your ear. Sir, I say to you, it
is thought you are false knaves.

BORACHIO Sir, I say to you we are none.

DOGBERRY Well, stand aside. 'Fore God, they are both
in a tale. Have you writ down that they are none? 32

SEXTON Master Constable, you go not the way to examine. You must call forth the watch that are their ac-
cusers.

DOGBERRY Yea, marry, that's the eftest way. Let the 36
watch come forth. Masters, I charge you in the
Prince's name accuse these men.

SEACOAL This man said, sir, that Don John, the Prince's
brother, was a villain.

DOGBERRY Write down Prince John a villain. Why, this
is flat perjury, to call a prince's brother villain.

BORACHIO Master Constable—

DOGBERRY Pray thee, fellow, peace. I do not like thy
look, I promise thee.

SEXTON What heard you him say else?

FIRST WATCH Marry, that he had received a thousand
ducats of Don John for accusing the Lady Hero wrong-
fully.

DOGBERRY Flat burglary as ever was committed.

VERGES Yea, by Mass, that it is. 51

SEXTON What else, fellow?

SEACOAL And that Count Claudio did mean, upon his
words, to disgrace Hero before the whole assembly,
and not marry her.

DOGBERRY O villain! Thou wilt be condemned into ev-
erlasting redemption for this. 57

SEXTON What else?

WATCH This is all. 59

---

26 witty clever, cunning **27 go about with** get the better of **32 in a
tale** in agreement **36 eftest** (Some sort of blunder for *easiest* or *deft-
est.*) **51 by mass** by the Mass **57 redemption** (Dogberry means *damnation.*) **59 s.p. Watch** (Perhaps both Seacoal and his partner speak.)

SEXTON And this is more, masters, than you can deny.
Prince John is this morning secretly stolen away. Hero
was in this manner accused, in this very manner
refused, and upon the grief of this suddenly died. Mas-
ter Constable, let these men be bound and brought to
Leonato's. I will go before and show him their exami-
nation.   [*Exit.*]
DOGBERRY Come, let them be opinioned.   67
VERGES Let them be in the hands—
CONRADE Off, coxcomb!
DOGBERRY God's my life, where's the sexton? Let him   70
write down the Prince's officer coxcomb. Come, bind
them. Thou naughty varlet!   72
CONRADE Away! You are an ass, you are an ass.
DOGBERRY Dost thou not suspect my place? Dost thou   74
not suspect my years? O, that he were here to write me
down an ass! But masters, remember that I am an ass;
though it be not written down, yet forget not that I am
an ass. No, thou villain, thou art full of piety, as shall   78
be proved upon thee by good witness. I am a wise
fellow, and, which is more, an officer, and, which is
more, a householder, and, which is more, as pretty a
piece of flesh as any is in Messina, and one that knows
the law, go to, and a rich fellow enough, go to, and a
fellow that hath had losses, and one that hath two
gowns and everything handsome about him. Bring
him away. O, that I had been writ down an ass!
                                        Exeunt.

❖

---

67 opinioned (For *pinioned.*) **70 God's** may God save **72 naughty**
wicked **74 suspect** (For *respect.*) **78 piety** (For *impiety.*)

5.1 *Enter Leonato and his brother [Antonio].*

ANTONIO
   If you go on thus, you will kill yourself;
   And 'tis not wisdom thus to second grief   2
   Against yourself.
LEONATO   I pray thee, cease thy counsel,
   Which falls into mine ears as profitless
   As water in a sieve. Give not me counsel,
   Nor let no comforter delight mine ear
   But such a one whose wrongs do suit with mine.   7
   Bring me a father that so loved his child,
   Whose joy of her is overwhelmed like mine,
   And bid him speak of patience;
   Measure his woe the length and breadth of mine,   11
   And let it answer every strain for strain,   12
   As thus for thus, and such a grief for such,
   In every lineament, branch, shape, and form;
   If such a one will smile and stroke his beard,
   Bid sorrow wag, cry "hem!" when he should groan,   16
   Patch grief with proverbs, make misfortune drunk   17
   With candle wasters, bring him yet to me   18
   And I of him will gather patience.
   But there is no such man. For, brother, men
   Can counsel and speak comfort to that grief
   Which they themselves not feel; but tasting it,
   Their counsel turns to passion, which before
   Would give preceptial medicine to rage,   24
   Fetter strong madness in a silken thread,
   Charm ache with air and agony with words.   26
   No, no, 'tis all men's office to speak patience   27
   To those that wring under the load of sorrow,   28
   But no man's virtue nor sufficiency   29
   To be so moral when he shall endure   30

5.1. Location: Near Leonato's house.
2 second assist, encourage   **7 suit with** match   **11 Measure his** let his
woe equal in scope   **12 strain** strong impulse of the mind   **16 wag** be off.
cry "hem" i.e., clear the throat as before some wordy speech   **17 drunk**
i.e., insensible to pain   **18 candle wasters** those who waste candles by late
study, bookworms, moral philosophers   **24 preceptial** consisting of pre-
cepts   **26 air** mere breath, words   **27 office** duty   **28 wring** writhe
29 sufficiency ability, power   **30 moral** prone to moralizing

The like himself. Therefore give me no counsel.
My griefs cry louder than advertisement.   32

ANTONIO
Therein do men from children nothing differ.

LEONATO
I pray thee, peace. I will be flesh and blood;
For there was never yet philosopher
That could endure the toothache patiently,
However they have writ the style of gods   37
And made a push at chance and sufferance.   38

ANTONIO
Yet bend not all the harm upon yourself.
Make those that do offend you suffer too.

LEONATO
There thou speak'st reason. Nay, I will do so.
My soul doth tell me Hero is belied,
And that shall Claudio know; so shall the Prince
And all of them that thus dishonor her.

Enter Prince [Don Pedro] and Claudio.

ANTONIO
Here comes the Prince and Claudio hastily.

DON PEDRO
Good e'en, good e'en.

CLAUDIO   Good day to both of you.

LEONATO
Hear you, my lords—

DON PEDRO   We have some haste, Leonato.

LEONATO
Some haste, my lord! Well, fare you well, my lord.
Are you so hasty now? Well, all is one.   49

DON PEDRO
Nay, do not quarrel with us, good old man.

ANTONIO
If he could right himself with quarreling,
Some of us would lie low.

CLAUDIO   Who wrongs him?   52

---

32 advertisement advice, counsel   **37 writ the style of** written in language worthy of   **38 push at** defiance of.   **sufferance** suffering   **49 all is one** it makes no difference   **52 Some of us** i.e., Don Pedro and Claudio

LEONATO
Marry, thou dost wrong me, thou dissembler, thou!   53
Nay, never lay thy hand upon thy sword;
I fear thee not.
CLAUDIO   Marry, beshrew my hand   55
If it should give your age such cause of fear.
In faith, my hand meant nothing to my sword.   57
LEONATO
Tush, tush, man, never fleer and jest at me.   58
I speak not like a dotard nor a fool,
As under privilege of age to brag
What I have done being young or what would do
Were I not old. Know, Claudio, to thy head,   62
Thou hast so wronged mine innocent child and me
That I am forced to lay my reverence by,   64
And with gray hairs and bruise of many days
Do challenge thee to trial of a man.   66
I say thou hast belied mine innocent child.
Thy slander hath gone through and through her heart,
And she lies buried with her ancestors—
O, in a tomb where never scandal slept,
Save this of hers, framed by thy villainy!   71
CLAUDIO
My villainy?
LEONATO   Thine, Claudio, thine, I say.
DON PEDRO
You say not right, old man.
LEONATO   My lord, my lord,
I'll prove it on his body if he dare,
Despite his nice fence and his active practice,   75
His May of youth and bloom of lustihood.   76
CLAUDIO
Away! I will not have to do with you.
LEONATO
Canst thou so daff me? Thou hast killed my child.   78
If thou kill'st me, boy, thou shalt kill a man.

53 thou (Used contemptuously instead of the more polite *you*.)
55 beshrew curse   **57 my . . . sword** I had no intention of using my
sword   **58 fleer** sneer, jeer   **62 head** i.e., face   **64 my reverence** i.e., the
reverence due old age   **66 trial of a man** manly contest, i.e., duel
71 framed devised   **75 nice fence** dexterous swordsmanship. (Said contemptuously.)   **76 lustihood** bodily vigor   **78 daff** doff, put or turn aside

ANTONIO
  He shall kill two of us, and men indeed.
  But that's no matter; let him kill one first.
  Win me and wear me! Let him answer me.   82
  Come follow me, boy. Come, sir boy, come follow me,
  Sir boy, I'll whip you from your foining fence!   84
  Nay, as I am a gentleman, I will.

LEONATO   Brother—

ANTONIO
  Content yourself. God knows I loved my niece,   87
  And she is dead, slandered to death by villains,
  That dare as well answer a man indeed
  As I dare take a serpent by the tongue.
  Boys, apes, braggarts, Jacks, milksops!

LEONATO   Brother Antony—

ANTONIO
  Hold you content. What, man! I know them, yea,
  And what they weigh, even to the utmost scruple—   94
  Scambling, outfacing, fashionmonging boys,   95
  That lie and cog and flout, deprave and slander,   96
  Go anticly, show outward hideousness,   97
  And speak off half a dozen dangerous words   98
  How they might hurt their enemies, if they durst,
  And this is all.

LEONATO
  But, brother Antony—

ANTONIO   Come, 'tis no matter.
  Do not you meddle; let me deal in this.

DON PEDRO
  Gentlemen both, we will not wake your patience.   103
  My heart is sorry for your daughter's death;
  But, on my honor, she was charged with nothing
  But what was true and very full of proof.

LEONATO   My lord, my lord—

DON PEDRO   I will not hear you.

---

82 Win . . . me (A proverbial expression, used as a challenge, meaning he'll have to overcome me before he can claim me as a prize.) **answer me** i.e., in a duel **84 foining** thrusting **87 Content yourself** i.e., don't try to stop me **94 scruple** small measure of weight **95 Scambling . . . boys** contentious, swaggering, dandified boys **96 cog** cheat. **deprave** defame, traduce **97 anticly** fantastically dressed. **hideousness** frightening appearance **98 dangerous** threatening, haughty **103 wake your patience** put your patience to any further test

LEONATO

  No? Come, brother, away! I will be heard.

ANTONIO

  And shall, or some of us will smart for it.   110

           Exeunt ambo [*Leonato and Antonio*].

  Enter Benedick.

DON PEDRO

  See, see, here comes the man we went to seek.

CLAUDIO Now, signor, what news?

BENEDICK Good day, my lord.

DON PEDRO Welcome, signor. You are almost come to part almost a fray.

CLAUDIO We had like to have had our two noses 116 snapped off with two old men without teeth.

DON PEDRO Leonato and his brother. What think'st thou? Had we fought, I doubt we should have been 119 too young for them.

BENEDICK In a false quarrel there is no true valor. I came to seek you both.

CLAUDIO We have been up and down to seek thee, for we are high-proof melancholy and would fain have it 124 beaten away. Wilt thou use thy wit?

BENEDICK It is in my scabbard. Shall I draw it?

DON PEDRO Dost thou wear thy wit by thy side?

CLAUDIO Never any did so, though very many have been beside their wit. I will bid thee draw, as we do 129 the minstrels, draw to pleasure us. 130

DON PEDRO As I am an honest man, he looks pale. Art thou sick, or angry?

CLAUDIO What, courage, man! What though care killed a cat, thou hast mettle enough in thee to kill care.

BENEDICK Sir, I shall meet your wit in the career, an you 135 charge it against me. I pray you, choose another sub- 136 ject.

---

110 s.d. ambo both **116 We had . . . had** we almost had **119 doubt** fear, suspect **124 high-proof** to the highest degree. **fain** gladly
129 beside their wit out of their wits (playing on *by thy side* in l. 127)
130 draw (1) draw your weapon (2) draw a bow across a musical instrument **135 career** short gallop at full speed (as in a tourney)
136 charge level (as a weapon)

CLAUDIO   Nay, then, give him another staff. This last 138
was broke 'cross.   139

DON PEDRO   By this light, he changes more and more. I
think he be angry indeed.

CLAUDIO   If he be, he knows how to turn his girdle.   142

BENEDICK   Shall I speak a word in your ear?

CLAUDIO   God bless me from a challenge!

BENEDICK [*Aside to Claudio*]   You are a villain. I jest not;
I will make it good how you dare, with what you dare,
and when you dare. Do me right, or I will protest your 147
cowardice. You have killed a sweet lady, and her death
shall fall heavy on you. Let me hear from you.

CLAUDIO   Well, I will meet you, so I may have good
cheer.

DON PEDRO   What, a feast, a feast?

CLAUDIO   I' faith, I thank him, he hath bid me to a calf's 153
head and a capon, the which if I do not carve most   154
curiously, say my knife's naught. Shall I not find a   155
woodcock too?   156

BENEDICK   Sir, your wit ambles well; it goes easily.   157

DON PEDRO   I'll tell thee how Beatrice praised thy wit the
other day. I said thou hadst a fine wit. "True," said
she, "a fine little one." "No," said I, "a great wit."
"Right," says she, "a great gross one." "Nay," said I,
"a good wit." "Just," said she, "it hurts nobody."
"Nay," said I, "the gentleman is wise." "Certain," said
she, "a wise gentleman." "Nay," said I, "he hath the 164
tongues." "That I believe," said she, "for he swore a 165
thing to me on Monday night which he forswore on
Tuesday morning. There's a double tongue; there's
two tongues." Thus did she, an hour together, trans- 168
shape thy particular virtues. Yet at last she concluded 169
with a sigh, thou wast the proper'st man in Italy.   170

---

138 staff spear shaft   **139 broke 'cross** i.e., broken by clumsily allowing the
spear to break crosswise against his opponent's shield. (In other words,
Claudio accuses Benedick of having failed in his sally of wit.)   **142 turn his
girdle** i.e., find harmless outlet for his anger (? A proverbial expression of
uncertain meaning.)   **147 Do me right** give me satisfaction.   **protest** proclaim before witnesses   **153–156 calf's head, capon, woodcock** (Used as
types of stupidity.)   **155 curiously** daintily.   **naught** good for nothing
157 ambles i.e., it does not gallop   **164 a wise gentleman** i.e., an old fool
164–165 hath the tongues masters several languages   **168–169 trans-
shape** distort, turn the wrong side out   **170 proper'st** handsomest

CLAUDIO For the which she wept heartily and said she
  cared not.

DON PEDRO Yea, that she did, but yet for all that, an if
  she did not hate him deadly, she would love him
  dearly. The old man's daughter told us all.

CLAUDIO All, all. And, moreover, God saw him when 176
  he was hid in the garden.   177

DON PEDRO But when shall we set the savage bull's
  horns on the sensible Benedick's head?

CLAUDIO Yea, and text underneath, "Here dwells Ben- 180
  edick the married man"?

BENEDICK Fare you well, boy. You know my mind. I
  will leave you now to your gossiplike humor. You
  break jests as braggarts do their blades, which, God 184
  be thanked, hurt not.—My lord, for your many courte-
  sies I thank you. I must discontinue your company.
  Your brother the bastard is fled from Messina. You
  have among you killed a sweet and innocent lady. For
  my Lord Lackbeard there, he and I shall meet, and till
  then peace be with him.   [Exit.]

DON PEDRO He is in earnest.

CLAUDIO In most profound earnest, and, I'll warrant
  you, for the love of Beatrice.

DON PEDRO And hath challenged thee?

CLAUDIO Most sincerely.

DON PEDRO What a pretty thing man is when he goes 196
  in his doublet and hose and leaves off his wit!   197

CLAUDIO He is then a giant to an ape; but then is an 198
  ape a doctor to such a man.   199

DON PEDRO But, soft you, let me be. Pluck up, my heart, 200
  and be sad. Did he not say my brother was fled?   201

  *Enter Constables, [Dogberry and Verges, and the
  Watch, with] Conrade and Borachio.*

176–177 God . . . garden (Alluding to the trick played on Benedick to love
Beatrice, and also to Genesis 3:8.)   **180 text** (In 1.1.251–256, Benedick
vowed that if he were ever to fall in love, his friends might set a bull's
horns on his head and label him "Benedick the married man.")   **184 as
. . . blades** i.e., as braggarts furtively damage their blades to make it
appear they have been fighting fiercely   **196–197 goes . . . wit** goes about
fully dressed but forgets to equip himself with good sense   **198–199 He
. . . man** he is superior to an ape in stature, but an ape is superior to him
in wisdom. (A doctor is a scholar.)   **200 soft you** wait a minute, not so
fast   **200–201 Pluck . . . sad** collect yourself, my mind, and be serious

DOGBERRY   Come you, sir. If Justice cannot tame you,
she shall ne'er weigh more reasons in her balance.   203
Nay, an you be a cursing hypocrite once, you must be
looked to.

DON PEDRO   How now, two of my brother's men
bound? Borachio one!

CLAUDIO   Hearken after their offense, my lord.   208

DON PEDRO   Officers, what offense have these men
done?

DOGBERRY   Marry, sir, they have committed false report;
moreover, they have spoken untruths; secondarily,
they are slanders; sixth and lastly, they have belied a   213
lady; thirdly, they have verified unjust things; and to
conclude, they are lying knaves.

DON PEDRO   First, I ask thee what they have done;
thirdly, I ask thee what's their offense; sixth and lastly,
why they are committed; and to conclude, what you
lay to their charge.

CLAUDIO   Rightly reasoned, and in his own division;
and, by my troth, there's one meaning well suited.   221

DON PEDRO   Who have you offended, masters, that you
are thus bound to your answer? This learned constable   223
is too cunning to be understood. What's your offense?

BORACHIO   Sweet Prince, let me go no farther to mine
answer. Do you hear me, and let this count kill me. I
have deceived even your very eyes. What your wisdoms could not discover, these shallow fools have
brought to light, who in the night overheard me con-
fessing to this man how Don John your brother in-   230
censed me to slander the Lady Hero, how you were   231
brought into the orchard and saw me court Margaret
in Hero's garments, how you disgraced her when you
should marry her. My villainy they have upon record,
which I had rather seal with my death than repeat over
to my shame. The lady is dead upon mine and my   236

---

203 ne'er . . . balance never again weigh arguments of reason in her
scales. (But the pronunciation of *reason* as "raisin" invokes the comic
image of a shopkeeper weighing produce.)   **208 Hearken after** inquire
into   **213 slanders** (For *slanderers.*)   **221 well suited** put into many
different dresses   **223 bound** (playing on the meanings "pinioned" and
"headed for a destination").   **answer** trial, account   **230–231 incensed**
incited   **236 upon** in consequence of

master's false accusation; and, briefly, I desire nothing
but the reward of a villain.

DON PEDRO [*To Claudio*]
Runs not this speech like iron through your blood?

CLAUDIO
I have drunk poison whiles he uttered it.

DON PEDRO
But did my brother set thee on to this?

BORACHIO   Yea, and paid me richly for the practice of it.   242

DON PEDRO
He is composed and framed of treachery,
And fled he is upon this villainy.

CLAUDIO
Sweet Hero! Now thy image doth appear
In the rare semblance that I loved it first.   246

DOGBERRY   Come, bring away the plaintiffs. By this   247
time our sexton hath reformed Signor Leonato of the   248
matter. And, masters, do not forget to specify, when   249
time and place shall serve, that I am an ass.

VERGES   Here, here comes Master Signor Leonato, and
the sexton too.

> *Enter Leonato, his brother [Antonio], and the*
> *Sexton.*

LEONATO
Which is the villain? Let me see his eyes,
That when I note another man like him
I may avoid him. Which of these is he?

BORACHIO
If you would know your wronger, look on me.

LEONATO
Art thou the slave that with thy breath hast killed
Mine innocent child?

BORACHIO   Yea, even I alone.

LEONATO
No, not so, villain, thou beliest thyself.
Here stand a pair of honorable men—   260
A third is fled—that had a hand in it.

---

242 practice execution   **246 rare semblance** splendid likeness   **247 plaintiffs** (For *defendants*.)   **248 reformed** (For *informed*.)   **249 specify** (For
testify?)   **260 honorable men** i.e., Don Pedro and Claudio, men of rank

I thank you, princes, for my daughter's death.
Record it with your high and worthy deeds.
'Twas bravely done, if you bethink you of it.

CLAUDIO
I know not how to pray your patience,
Yet I must speak. Choose your revenge yourself;
Impose me to what penance your invention   267
Can lay upon my sin. Yet sinned I not
But in mistaking.

DON PEDRO   By my soul, nor I.
And yet, to satisfy this good old man,
I would bend under any heavy weight
That he'll enjoin me to.

LEONATO
I cannot bid you bid my daughter live—
That were impossible—but, I pray you both,
Possess the people in Messina here   275
How innocent she died; and if your love
Can labor aught in sad invention,   277
Hang her an epitaph upon her tomb
And sing it to her bones—sing it tonight.
Tomorrow morning come you to my house,
And since you could not be my son-in-law,
Be yet my nephew. My brother hath a daughter,
Almost the copy of my child that's dead,
And she alone is heir to both of us.   284
Give her the right you should have given her cousin,   285
And so dies my revenge.

CLAUDIO   O noble sir,
Your overkindness doth wring tears from me!
I do embrace your offer; and dispose   288
For henceforth of poor Claudio.   289

LEONATO
Tomorrow then I will expect your coming;
Tonight I take my leave. This naughty man   291
Shall face to face be brought to Margaret,

---

267 Impose me to impose on me   **275 Possess** inform   **277 aught** to any
extent   **284 heir to both** (He overlooks Antonio's son mentioned in
1.2.2.)   **285 right** equitable treatment (quibbling on *rite*, "ceremony")
288 dispose you may dispose   **289 For henceforth** for the future
291 naughty wicked

Who I believe was packed in all this wrong,   293
Hired to it by your brother.

BORACHIO   No, by my soul, she was not,
Nor knew not what she did when she spoke to me,
But always hath been just and virtuous
In anything that I do know by her.   298

DOGBERRY   Moreover, sir, which indeed is not under   299
white and black, this plaintiff here, the offender, did   300
call me ass. I beseech you, let it be remembered in his
punishment. And also, the watch heard them talk of
one Deformed. They say he wears a key in his ear and   303
a lock hanging by it and borrows money in God's   304
name, the which he hath used so long and never paid   305
that now men grow hardhearted and will lend noth-
ing for God's sake. Pray you, examine him upon that
point.

LEONATO   I thank thee for thy care and honest pains.

DOGBERRY   Your worship speaks like a most thankful
and reverend youth, and I praise God for you.

LEONATO   There's for thy pains.   [*He gives money.*]

DOGBERRY   God save the foundation!   313

LEONATO   Go, I discharge thee of thy prisoner, and I
thank thee.

DOGBERRY   I leave an arrant knave with your worship,
which I beseech your worship to correct yourself, for
the example of others. God keep your worship! I wish
your worship well. God restore you to health! I humbly give you leave to depart; and if a merry meeting   320
may be wished, God prohibit it! Come, neighbor.   321
          [*Exeunt Dogberry and Verges.*]

LEONATO
Until tomorrow morning, lords, farewell.

ANTONIO
Farewell, my lords. We look for you tomorrow.

---

293 packed involved as an accomplice   **298 by** concerning
299–300 under . . . black written down in black and white   **303–304 key
. . . by it** (This is what Dogberry has made out of the lovelock mentioned
in 3.3.167.)   **304–305 in God's name** (A phrase of the professional
beggar.)   **313 God . . . foundation** (A formula of those who received alms
at religious houses or charitable foundations.)   **320 give you leave** (For
ask your leave.)   **321 prohibit** (For *permit.*)

DON PEDRO
  We will not fail.
CLAUDIO   Tonight I'll mourn with Hero.
LEONATO [*To the Watch*]
  Bring you these fellows on.—We'll talk with Margaret,
  How her acquaintance grew with this lewd fellow.   326
                                Exeunt [*separately*].

                    ✤

5.2   *Enter Benedick and Margaret,* [*meeting*].

BENEDICK Pray thee, sweet Mistress Margaret, de-
  serve well at my hands by helping me to the speech of
  Beatrice.
MARGARET Will you then write me a sonnet in praise of
  my beauty?
BENEDICK In so high a style, Margaret, that no man liv-   6
  ing shall come over it, for in most comely truth thou   7
  deservest it.
MARGARET To have no man come over me! Why, shall
  I always keep below stairs?   10
BENEDICK Thy wit is as quick as the greyhound's
  mouth; it catches.
MARGARET And yours as blunt as the fencer's foils,
  which hit but hurt not.
BENEDICK A most manly wit, Margaret; it will not hurt
  a woman. And so, I pray thee, call Beatrice. I give thee   16
  the bucklers.   17
MARGARET Give us the swords; we have bucklers of
  our own.
BENEDICK If you use them, Margaret, you must put in

---

326 lewd wicked, worthless

**5.2. Location: Leonato's garden (?) (At the scene's end, Leonato's house
is some distance away.)**
6 style (1) poetic style (2) stile, stairs over a fence   **7 come over** (1) excel
beyond (2) traverse, as one would cross a stile (3) in Margaret's next
speech, the phrase is taken to mean "mount sexually."   **comely** good
(with an allusion to Margaret's beauty)   **10 keep below stairs** dwell in
the servants' quarters   **16–17 I . . . bucklers** i.e., I acknowledge myself
beaten (in repartee). (Bucklers are shields with spikes [pikes] in their
centers; Margaret uses the word in a bawdy sense in her reply.)

the pikes with a vice, and they are dangerous weapons 21
for maids.

MARGARET   Well, I will call Beatrice to you, who I think
hath legs.   *Exit Margaret.*

BENEDICK   And therefore will come.

[*Sings.*]   "The god of love,   26
            That sits above,
      And knows me, and knows me,
            How pitiful I deserve—"   29

I mean in singing; but in loving, Leander the good 30
swimmer, Troilus the first employer of panders, and a 31
whole bookful of these quondam carpetmongers, 32
whose names yet run smoothly in the even road of a
blank verse, why, they were never so truly turned over 34
and over as my poor self in love. Marry, I cannot show 35
it in rhyme; I have tried. I can find out no rhyme to
"lady" but "baby," an innocent rhyme; for "scorn," 37
"horn," a hard rhyme; for "school," "fool," a babbling 38
rhyme; very ominous endings. No, I was not born under a rhyming planet, nor I cannot woo in festival 40
terms.   41

     Enter Beatrice.

Sweet Beatrice, wouldst thou come when I called thee?

BEATRICE   Yea, signor, and depart when you bid me.

BENEDICK   O, stay but till then!

BEATRICE   "Then" is spoken; fare you well now. And
yet, ere I go, let me go with that I came, which is, with 46
knowing what hath passed between you and Claudio.

BENEDICK   Only foul words; and thereupon I will kiss
thee.

---

21 pikes spikes in the center of a shield.   **vice** screw   **26–29 The god
. . . deserve** (The beginning of an old song by William Elderton.)
29 How . . . deserve how I deserve pity. (But Benedick uses the phrase
to mean "how little I deserve.")   **30 Leander** lover of Hero of Sestos; he
swam the Hellespont nightly to see her until he drowned   **31 Troilus**
lover of Cressida, whose affair was assisted by her uncle Pandarus
32 quondam former, old-time.   **carpetmongers** (A scornful term for
"ladies' men," derived from their presence in the carpeted boudoirs of
their lovers.)   **34–35 over and over** i.e., head over heels   **37 innocent**
childish   **38 hard** (1) exact (2) unpleasant, because of the association
with cuckold's horns   **40–41 festival terms** elevated language   **46 that I
came** what I came for

BEATRICE   Foul words is but foul wind, and foul wind is but foul breath, and foul breath is noisome; therefore 51 I will depart unkissed.

BENEDICK   Thou hast frighted the word out of his right 53 sense, so forcible is thy wit. But I must tell thee plainly, Claudio undergoes my challenge; and either I 55 must shortly hear from him, or I will subscribe him a 56 coward. And I pray thee now tell me, for which of my bad parts didst thou first fall in love with me?

BEATRICE   For them all together, which maintained so politic a state of evil that they will not admit any good 60 part to intermingle with them. But for which of my good parts did you first suffer love for me? 62

BENEDICK   Suffer love! A good epithet! I do suffer love 63 indeed, for I love thee against my will.

BEATRICE   In spite of your heart, I think. Alas, poor heart, if you spite it for my sake, I will spite it for yours, for I will never love that which my friend hates.

BENEDICK   Thou and I are too wise to woo peaceably.

BEATRICE   It appears not in this confession. There's not 69 one wise man among twenty that will praise himself.

BENEDICK   An old, an old instance, Beatrice, that lived in 71 the time of good neighbors. If a man do not erect in 72 this age his own tomb ere he dies, he shall live no 73 longer in monument than the bell rings and the 74 widow weeps. 75

BEATRICE   And how long is that, think you?

BENEDICK   Question: why, an hour in clamor and a 77 quarter in rheum. Therefore is it most expedient for 78 the wise, if Don Worm, his conscience, find no im- 79 pediment to the contrary, to be the trumpet of his own

---

51 noisome noxious   **53 his** its   **55 undergoes** bears   **56 subscribe** formally proclaim in writing   **60 politic** prudently governed   **62 suffer** (1) experience (2) feel the pain of   **63 epithet** expression   **69 It . . . confession** i.e., you don't show your wisdom in praising yourself for being wise   **71 instance** proverb   **72 time . . . neighbors** good old times (when one's neighbors spoke well of one)   **73–75 he shall . . . weeps** i.e., he will be memorialized only during the (brief) time of the funeral service and the official mourning   **77 Question** i.e., an easy question, which I will answer as follows.   **clamor** noise (of the bell)   **78 rheum** tears (of the widow)   **79 Don . . . conscience** (The action of the conscience was traditionally described as the gnawing of a worm; cf. Mark 9:48.)

virtues, as I am to myself. So much for praising myself, who, I myself will bear witness, is praiseworthy. And now tell me, how doth your cousin?

BEATRICE   Very ill.

BENEDICK   And how do you?

BEATRICE   Very ill too.

BENEDICK   Serve God, love me, and mend. There will I leave you too, for here comes one in haste.

Enter Ursula.

URSULA   Madam, you must come to your uncle. Yonder's old coil at home. It is proved my Lady Hero hath 90 been falsely accused, the Prince and Claudio mightily abused, and Don John is the author of all, who is fled 92 and gone. Will you come presently?   93

BEATRICE   Will you go hear this news, signor?

BENEDICK   I will live in thy heart, die in thy lap, and be 95 buried in thy eyes; and moreover I will go with thee to thy uncle's.   *Exeunt.*

❖

5.3   *Enter Claudio, Prince [Don Pedro, Balthasar], and three or four with tapers.*

CLAUDIO   Is this the monument of Leonato?

A LORD   It is, my lord.

CLAUDIO [*Reading from a scroll*]

Epitaph.

"Done to death by slanderous tongues
        Was the Hero that here lies.
Death, in guerdon of her wrongs,   5
        Gives her fame which never dies.
So the life that died with shame
Lives in death with glorious fame."

90 old coil great confusion   **92 abused** deceived   **93 presently** immediately   **95 die** (with the common connotation of "experience sexual climax")

5.3. Location: A churchyard.
5 guerdon recompense

Hang thou there upon the tomb,
Praising her when I am dumb.

                        [He hangs up the scroll.]
Now, music, sound, and sing your solemn hymn.

                     Song.

BALTHASAR
          Pardon, goddess of the night,   12
          Those that slew thy virgin knight;
          For the which, with songs of woe,
          Round about her tomb they go.
             Midnight, assist our moan;
             Help us to sigh and groan,
                Heavily, heavily.
             Graves, yawn and yield your dead,
             Till death be utterèd,   20
                Heavily, heavily.
CLAUDIO
Now, unto thy bones good night!
Yearly will I do this rite.
DON PEDRO
Good morrow, masters. Put your torches out.
  The wolves have preyed; and look, the gentle day, 25
Before the wheels of Phoebus, round about 26
  Dapples the drowsy east with spots of gray.
Thanks to you all, and leave us. Fare you well.
CLAUDIO
Good morrow, masters. Each his several way.
DON PEDRO
Come, let us hence, and put on other weeds, 30
  And then to Leonato's we will go.
CLAUDIO
And Hymen now with luckier issue speed 's 32
  Than this for whom we rendered up this woe.

                           Exeunt.

                ❖

---

12 goddess of the night i.e., Diana, moon goddess, patroness of chastity **20 utterèd** fully expressed **25 have preyed** i.e., have ceased preying **26 wheels of Phoebus** i.e., chariot of the sun god **30 weeds** garments **32 Hymen** god of marriage. **speed 's** favor or speed us

5.4   *Enter Leonato, Benedick, [Beatrice], Margaret,*
Ursula, Old Man [Antonio], Friar [Francis],
Hero.

FRIAR
  Did I not tell you she was innocent?

LEONATO
  So are the Prince and Claudio, who accused her
  Upon the error that you heard debated.   3
  But Margaret was in some fault for this,
  Although against her will, as it appears   5
  In the true course of all the question.   6

ANTONIO
  Well, I am glad that all things sorts so well.   7

BENEDICK
  And so am I, being else by faith enforced   8
  To call young Claudio to a reckoning for it.

LEONATO
  Well, daughter, and you gentlewomen all,
  Withdraw into a chamber by yourselves,
  And when I send for you, come hither masked.
  The Prince and Claudio promised by this hour
  To visit me. You know your office, brother: 14
  You must be father to your brother's daughter,
  And give her to young Claudio.   *Exeunt Ladies.*

ANTONIO
  Which I will do with confirmed countenance.   17

BENEDICK
  Friar, I must entreat your pains, I think.   18

FRIAR   To do what, signor?

BENEDICK
  To bind me or undo me—one of them.   20
  Signor Leonato, truth it is, good signor,
  Your niece regards me with an eye of favor.

LEONATO
  That eye my daughter lent her. 'Tis most true.   23

5.4. Location: Leonato's house.
3 Upon because of   **5 against her will** unintentionally   **6 question**
investigation   **7 sorts** turn out   **8 being else** since otherwise I would
be. **by faith** i.e., by my promise to Beatrice   **14 office** duty   **17 con-**
firmed countenance confident bearing   **18 entreat your pains** i.e.,
impose on you   **20 undo** (1) ruin (2) untie, unbind   **23 That . . . her**
(Alludes to Hero's role in coaxing Beatrice to love Benedick.)

BENEDICK
  And I do with an eye of love requite her.
LEONATO
  The sight whereof I think you had from me,   25
  From Claudio, and the Prince. But what's your will?   26
BENEDICK
  Your answer, sir, is enigmatical.
  But, for my will, my will is your good will   28
  May stand with ours, this day to be conjoined
  In the state of honorable marriage,
  In which, good Friar, I shall desire your help.
LEONATO
  My heart is with your liking.
FRIAR   And my help.
  Here comes the Prince and Claudio.

        *Enter Prince [Don Pedro] and Claudio, and two
        or three other.*

DON PEDRO
  Good morrow to this fair assembly.
LEONATO
  Good morrow, Prince; good morrow, Claudio.
  We here attend you. Are you yet determined   35
  Today to marry with my brother's daughter?
CLAUDIO
  I'll hold my mind, were she an Ethiope.
LEONATO
  Call her forth, brother. Here's the Friar ready.
                                    [*Exit Antonio.*]
DON PEDRO
  Good morrow, Benedick. Why, what's the matter,
  That you have such a February face,
  So full of frost, of storm, and cloudiness?
CLAUDIO
  I think he thinks upon the savage bull.   42
  Tush, fear not, man! We'll tip thy horns with gold,
  And all Europa shall rejoice at thee,   44

25-26 The sight ... Prince (Alludes to their role in coaxing Benedick to
love Beatrice.) **28 is** is that **35 yet** still **42 I ... bull** (A jocular remi-
niscence of the conversation in 1.1.250 ff.) **44 Europa** Europe

As once Europa did at lusty Jove   45
When he would play the noble beast in love.

BENEDICK
Bull Jove, sir, had an amiable low,
And some such strange bull leapt your father's cow
And got a calf in that same noble feat
Much like to you, for you have just his bleat.

    Enter [Leonato's] brother [Antonio], Hero,
    Beatrice, Margaret, Ursula, [the ladies masked].

CLAUDIO
For this I owe you. Here comes other reckonings.   51
Which is the lady I must seize upon?

ANTONIO
This same is she, and I do give you her.

CLAUDIO
Why, then she's mine. Sweet, let me see your face.

LEONATO
No, that you shall not, till you take her hand
Before this friar and swear to marry her.

CLAUDIO
Give me your hand before this holy friar.
I am your husband, if you like of me.   58

HERO [*Unmasking*]
And when I lived, I was your other wife;
And when you loved, you were my other husband.

CLAUDIO
Another Hero!

HERO   Nothing certainer.
One Hero died defiled, but I do live,
And surely as I live, I am a maid.

DON PEDRO
The former Hero! Hero that is dead!

LEONATO
She died, my lord, but whiles her slander lived.   65

FRIAR
All this amazement can I qualify,   66

45 Europa a princess whom Jove approached in the form of a white bull
and bore on his back through the sea to Crete   **51 I owe you** i.e., I'll pay
you back later (for calling me a calf and a bastard child of Jove).   **other
reckonings** i.e., other matters to be settled first   **58 like of** care for
65 but whiles only while   **66 qualify** moderate

When, after that the holy rites are ended,
I'll tell you largely of fair Hero's death.   68
Meantime let wonder seem familiar,   69
And to the chapel let us presently.   70

BENEDICK
Soft and fair, Friar. Which is Beatrice?

BEATRICE [*Unmasking*]
I answer to that name. What is your will?

BENEDICK
Do not you love me?

BEATRICE   Why, no, no more than reason.

BENEDICK
Why, then your uncle and the Prince and Claudio
Have been deceived. They swore you did.

BEATRICE
Do not you love me?

BENEDICK   Troth, no, no more than reason.

BEATRICE
Why, then my cousin Margaret and Ursula
Are much deceived, for they did swear you did.

BENEDICK
They swore that you were almost sick for me.

BEATRICE
They swore that you were well-nigh dead for me.

BENEDICK
'Tis no such matter. Then you do not love me?

BEATRICE
No, truly, but in friendly recompense.

LEONATO
Come, cousin, I am sure you love the gentleman.

CLAUDIO
And I'll be sworn upon 't that he loves her;
For here's a paper written in his hand,
A halting sonnet of his own pure brain,   86
Fashioned to Beatrice.   [*He shows a paper.*]

HERO   And here's another
Writ in my cousin's hand, stol'n from her pocket,

---

68 largely at large, in full   **69 let . . . familiar** treat these marvels as
ordinary matters   **70 let us presently** let us go at once   **86 his own
pure** purely his own

Containing her affection unto Benedick.

[She shows another paper.]

BENEDICK   A miracle! Here's our own hands against our 90
hearts. Come, I will have thee, but by this light I take 91
thee for pity.

BEATRICE   I would not deny you, but by this good day,
I yield upon great persuasion, and partly to save your
life, for I was told you were in a consumption.

BENEDICK   Peace! I will stop your mouth. *[He kisses her.]*

DON PEDRO   How dost thou, Benedick, the married
man?

BENEDICK   I'll tell thee what, Prince: a college of wit- 99
crackers cannot flout me out of my humor. Dost thou
think I care for a satire or an epigram? No. If a man 101
will be beaten with brains, 'a shall wear nothing hand- 102
some about him. In brief, since I do purpose to marry, 103
I will think nothing to any purpose that the world can
say against it; and therefore never flout at me for what
I have said against it; for man is a giddy thing, and
this is my conclusion. For thy part, Claudio, I did
think to have beaten thee, but in that thou art like to
be my kinsman, live unbruised, and love my cousin.

CLAUDIO   I had well hoped thou wouldst have denied
Beatrice, that I might have cudgeled thee out of thy
single life, to make thee a double-dealer, which out of 112
question thou wilt be, if my cousin do not look ex- 113
ceeding narrowly to thee. 114

BENEDICK   Come, come, we are friends. Let's have a
dance ere we are married, that we may lighten our
own hearts and our wives' heels.

LEONATO   We'll have dancing afterward.

BENEDICK   First, of my word! Therefore play, music. 119
Prince, thou art sad. Get thee a wife, get thee a wife.
There is no staff more reverend than one tipped with 121
horn. 122

90–91 against our hearts i.e., to prove our hearts guilty as charged   **99 college** assembly   **101–103 If . . . him** i.e., if a man allows himself to be cowed by ridicule, he'll never dare dress handsomely or do anything conspicuous that will draw attention   **112 a double-dealer** (1) a married man (2) a deceiver, adulterer   **113–114 look . . . narrowly** pay close attention   **119 of** on   **121–122 tipped with horn** (Alludes to the usual joke about cuckolds.)

Enter Messenger.

MESSENGER
  My lord, your brother John is ta'en in flight
  And brought with armèd men back to Messina.
BENEDICK   Think not on him till tomorrow. I'll devise
  thee brave punishments for him. Strike up, pipers.   126
                              Dance. [Exeunt.]

❖

126 brave fine

Date and Text

"The Commedie of muche A doo about nothing a booke" was entered in the Stationers' Register, the official record book of the London Company of Stationers (booksellers and printers), on August 4, 1600, along with *As You Like It, Henry V,* and Ben Jonson's *Every Man in His Humor,* all marked as plays of "My lord chamberlens men" (Shakespeare's acting company) and all "to be staied"—that is, not published without further permission. Earlier in the same memorandum, written on a spare page in the Register, occurs the name of the printer James Roberts, whose registration of *The Merchant of Venice* in 1598 was similarly stayed pending further permission to publish. Evidently the Chamberlain's men were attempting to prevent unauthorized publication of these very popular plays. They were too late to forestall the appearance of a bad quarto of *Henry V* in August of 1600, but they did manage to control release of the others. *Much Ado about Nothing* appeared later that same year in a seemingly authorized version:

> Much adoe about Nothing. *As it hath been sundrie times publikely* acted by the right honourable, the Lord Chamberlaine his seruants. *Written by William Shakespeare.* LONDON Printed by V. S. [Valentine Sims] for Andrew Wise, and William Aspley. 1600.

Once thought to have been set up from a theatrical promptbook and then used itself in the theater as a promptbook before serving as copy for the First Folio of 1623, this 1600 quarto text is now generally regarded as having been set from Shakespeare's own manuscript. The names of the actors Will Kempe and Richard Cowley appear among the speech prefixes in 4.2, indicating that an actual stage production was very close at hand, but other irregularities in speech prefixes and scene headings read more like a manuscript in the last stages of revision than a promptbook for a finished production. The Folio text was based on this 1600 quarto, lightly annotated with reference to the promptbook but providing little in the way of new readings other than the correction of obvious error.

Francis Meres does not mention the play in September of 1598 in his *Palladis Tamia: Wit's Treasury* (a slender volume on contemporary literature and art; valuable because it lists most of Shakespeare's plays that existed at that time), unless (and this seems unlikely) it is his *"Loue labours wonne."* Will Kempe, who played Dogberry, left the Chamberlain's men in 1599. The likeliest date, then, is the winter of 1598–1599, though publication was not until 1600.

Textual Notes

These textual notes are not a historical collation, either of the early quarto and the early folios or of more recent editions; they are simply a record of departures in this edition from the copy text. The reading adopted in this edition appears in boldface, followed by the rejected reading from the copy text, i.e., the quarto of 1600. Only a few major alterations in punctuation are noted. Changes in lineation are not indicated, nor are some minor and obvious typographical errors.

Abbreviations used:
Q the quarto of 1600
s.d. stage direction
s.p. speech prefix

Copy text: the quarto of 1600.

1.1. s.d. Messina Messina, Innogen, his wife **2 Pedro** Peter [also in l. 9] **194 s.d. Pedro** Pedro, Iohn the bastard

1.2. 3 s.p. [and elsewhere] Antonio Old **6 event** euents **24 skill** shill

1.3. 51 on one **70 s.d. Exeunt** exit

2.1 s.d. Hero his wife, Hero **Ursula** [Q adds "and a kinsman"] **2 s.p. [and elsewhere] Antonio** brother **37 bearward** Berrord **44 Peter, for the heavens; Peter:** for the heauens, **67 hear** here **79 s.d. and Don** or dumb **80 about** about **94 s.p. Balthasar** Bene [also at ll. 97 and 99] **201 s.d. Leonato** Leonato, Iohn and Borachio, and Conrade **311 s.p. [and elsewhere] Don Pedro** Prince **369 s.d. Exeunt** exit

2.3. 7 s.d. [at l. 5 in Q] 24 an and **35 s.d. Claudio** Claudio, Musicke **61 s.p. Balthasar** [not in Q] **139 us of** of vs

3.1. s.d. Ursula Vrsley **23 s.d. [at l. 25 in Q]**

3.2. 27 can cannot **51 s.p. Don Pedro** Bene **74 s.p. [and elsewhere] Don John** Bastard

3.3. 17 s.p. Seacoal Watch 2 [also at l. 27] **87 s.p. Seacoal** Watch [also at ll. 95, 105, 125] **161 s.p. Seacoal** Watch 1 [also at l. 165] **162 s.p. First Watch** Watch 2 [also at l. 169] **171 s.p. Seacoal** [missing in Q]

3.4. 17 in it

3.5. 2 s.p. [and elsewhere] Dogberry Const. Dog **7 s.p. [and elsewhere] Verges** Headb **9 off** of **50** [Q provides an "Exit" at this point]

4.1. 4 s.p. Friar Fran **202 princes** princesse

4.2. s.d. [Q reads "Enter the Constables, Borachio, and the Towne clearke in gownes."] **1 s.p. Dogberry** Keeper **2 s.p. [and elsewhere in this scene] Verges** Cowley **4 s.p. Dogberry Andrew** **9 s.p. [and elsewhere in this scene] Dogberry** Kemp **18 s.p. Conrade, Borachio** Both **39 Seacoal** Watch 1 [also at l. 53] **47 First Watch** Watch 2 **51 s.p. Verges** Const **67 s.p. [and elsewhere] Dogberry** Constable **69 s.p. Conrade** [missing in Q] **69 Off** of **73 s.p. Conrade** Couley **86 s.d. Exeunt** exit

5.1. 16 Bid And   **97 anticly** antiquely, and   **98 off** of   **179 on** one
201 s.d. [at l. 197 in Q]   **251 s.p. Verges** Con. 2

5.2. 41 s.d. [at l. 42 in Q]   **81 myself. So** my self so   **97 s.d. Exeunt** exit

5.3. 2 s.p. A Lord Lord   **3 s.p. Claudio** [missing in Q]   **10 dumb** dead
12 s.p. Balthasar [missing in Q]   **22 s.p. Claudio** Lo

5.4. 53 s.p. Antonio Leo   **96 s.p. Benedick** Leon

Shakespeare's Sources

Shakespeare's probable chief source for the Hero-Claudio plot of *Much Ado* was the twenty-second story from the *Novelle* of Matteo Bandello (Lucca, 1554). A French translation by François de Belleforest, in his *Histoires Tragiques* (1569 edition) was available to Shakespeare, as was the Italian original. The story of the maiden falsely accused was, however, much older than the story by Bandello. Perhaps the earliest version that has been found is the Greek romance *Chaereas and Callirrhoe,* fourth or fifth century A.D., in which the hero Chaereas, warned by envious rivals of his wife's purported infidelity, watches at dusk while an elegantly attired stranger is admitted by the maid to the house where Callirrhoe lives. Chaereas rushes in and strikes mistakenly at his wife in the dark, but is acquitted of murder when the maid confesses her part in a conspiracy to delude Chaereas. Callirrhoe is buried in a deathlike trance but awakens in time to be carried off by pirates. The story reappears in a fifteenth-century Spanish romance, *Tirante el Blanco,* in which the princess Blanche is courted seemingly by a repulsive black man. This Spanish version probably inspired the account in Canto 5 of Ludovico Ariosto's *Orlando Furioso* (1516), to which all subsequent Renaissance versions are ultimately indebted.

In Ariosto's account, as translated into English by Sir John Harington (1591), the narrator is Dalinda, maid to the virtuous Scottish princess Genevra. Dalinda tells how she has fallen guiltily in love with Polynesso, Duke of Albany, an evil man who often makes love to Dalinda in her mistress' rooms but who longs to marry Genevra himself. Consequently, Polynesso arranges for Genevra's noble Italian suitor, Ariodante, and Ariodante's brother Lurcanio, to witness the Duke's ascent to Genevra's window by a rope ladder. The woman who admits the Duke is of course not Genevra but Dalinda disguised as her mistress, having been duped into believing that the Duke merely wishes to satisfy his craving for Genevra by making love to her image. Lurcanio publicly accuses the innocent Genevra and offers to fight anyone who defends her cause (compare Claudio's quarrel with Leonato).

The evil Duke tries to get rid of Dalinda, but all is finally put to rights by Rinaldo (the hero of *Orlando Furioso*) and Ariodante. This account gives an unusually vivid motivation for the maid and the villain—a clearer motivation than in Shakespeare's play. A lost dramatic version, *Ariodante and Genevora*, was performed at the English court in 1583.

Shakespeare probably consulted not only Ariosto but also Edmund Spenser's *The Faerie Queene* (2.4), based on Ariosto. Spenser's emphasis is on the blind rage of Phedon, a young squire in love with Claribell. Phedon is tricked by his erstwhile friend Philemon and by Claribell's maid Pryene into believing Claribell false. Pryene's motive in dressing up as Claribell is to prove she is as beautiful as her mistress. When, after having slain Claribell for her supposed perfidy, Phedon learns the truth, he poisons Philemon and furiously pursues Pryene until he is utterly possessed by a mad frenzy.

Shakespeare's greatest debt is, however, to Bandello's story. Its text follows, somewhat excerpted, in a new translation. In a number of details the story is closer to Shakespeare's play than are those already discussed. Several names are substantially as in Shakespeare: the location is Messina, the father of the slandered bride is Lionato di' Lionati (compare Shakespeare's Leonato), and her lover is in the service of King Piero of Aragon (compare Don Pedro of Aragon). As in Shakespeare, a young knight (named Sir Timbreo) seeks the hand in marriage of his beloved (Fenicia) through the matchmaking offices of a noble emissary. The complication of this wooing is somewhat different in that Timbreo's friend Girondo also falls in love with Fenicia, but Girondo does then plot with a mischief-loving courtier (resembling Shakespeare's Don John) to poison Timbreo's mind against Fenicia, and Girondo thereupon escorts Timbreo to a garden where they see Girondo's servant, elegantly dressed, enter Fenicia's window. No maid takes part in the ruse, however, nor indeed is any woman seen at the window. When Fenicia is wrongly accused, she falls into a deathlike trance and is pronounced dead by a doctor, but is revived. Her father, believing in her innocence, sends her off to a country retreat and circulates the report that she is in fact dead. Soon both Timbreo and Girondo are stricken with remorse, Timbreo magnanimously spares his friend's life, and both

confess the truth to Fenicia's family. A year later, Timbreo
marries a wife chosen for him by Lionato, who turns out of
course to be Fenicia. Girondo marries her sister Belfiore.
This account does not provide any equivalent for Beatrice
and Benedick. Shakespeare enhances the Friar's role, and
provides a brother for Leonato. Claudio and Leonato are of
comparable social station in Shakespeare, whereas Bandello
makes a point of a difference in social class.

A lost play, *Panecia* (1574–1575), may have been based on
Bandello's work. One other version Shakespeare may have
known is George Whetstone's *The Rock of Regard* (1576),
based on Ariosto and Bandello. It contains a suggestive
parallel to Claudio's rejection of Hero in church. Various
Italian plays in the tradition of Luigi Pasqualigo's *Il Fedele*
(1579), and also a version perhaps by Anthony Munday,
Fedele and Fortunio (published 1585), are analogous in situation, though Shakespeare need not have known any of them.

For the Beatrice-Benedick plot no source has been discovered, apart from Shakespeare's own earlier fascination
with wit combat and candid wooing in *Love's Labor's Lost*
and *The Taming of the Shrew*. Nor has a plausible source
been found for Dogberry and the watch.

Novelle
Part One
By Matteo Bandello
Translated by David Bevington and Kate Bevington

NOVELLA TWENTY-TWO:
TIMBREO AND FENICIA

During the year of our salvation 1283, the people of Sicily,
no longer willing to put up with the domination of their
French overlords, massacred all of them on the island one
day at the hour of vespers, with unheard-of cruelty; thus
was the treachery ordered and carried out throughout the
island. They killed not only women and men of the French
nation but all Sicilian women who could be suspected of
being made pregnant by the French; on one and the same
day they cut the French throats, and then if any woman

was found pregnant by the French, she was killed without remorse. From this was born the despicable name of "Sicilian Vespers."

When King Piero of Aragon heard of this, he came at once with his army and took charge of the island, as Pope Nicholas III had urged him, declaring that the island belonged to him as husband of Constanza, daughter of King Manfred. King Piero held regal and magnificent court in Palermo several days, celebrating with great festivity his taking of the island. Then, hearing that King Carlo II, son of King Carlo I and possessor of the kingdom of Naples, was approaching by sea with a great army to chase him out of Sicily, he set out against him with the armed force of ships and galleys under his command. When they came together in combat, there was a great fray and cruel slaughter of many men. But in the end King Piero routed the army of King Carlo and took him prisoner. And the better to attend to military matters, he withdrew with all the court to Messina, since in that city one was closest to Italy and most quickly able to cross over into Calabria.

While he was there magnificently holding court, and all was joyful in honor of the victory he had won, and everyone was passing the time in feats of arms and in dancing, one of his knights, a baron, greatly esteemed and especially so by King Piero because he was so brave and had conducted himself so valiantly in the recent fighting, fell head over heels in love with a young lady, the daughter of Master Lionato de' Lionati, gentleman of Messina. She, more than any other lady in the whole country, was of gentle condition, attractive, and beautiful, and little by little the knight was so inflamed with desire of her that without the sweet sight of her he didn't even know how he could live. Now, the baron was called Timbreo di Cardona, and the young woman, Fenicia. He, because he had served King Piero by land and by sea since his youngest days, had been richly rewarded in many ways. Besides the countless gifts that were his, the King had recently given him the county of Colisano along with other lands, so that his income, over and above the allowance the King had already provided, came to more than twelve thousand ducats.

Signor Timbreo now began to pass daily in front of the young lady's house, thinking the day a blessed one whenever he saw her. Fenicia, being clever and sagacious for her age, soon guessed the motive of the knight's strolls. Now, it was well known that Signor Timbreo was one of the King's favorites and that few were valued in the court more highly than he, for which reason he was honored by one and all. Fenicia too, seeing in addition to all she had heard of him that he was well dressed in the courtly fashion, descended from a noble family, handsome, and well-mannered in appearance, began for her part to pay attention to him in an agreeable manner and salute him discreetly. The knight's ardor grew day by day, and the more he gazed on her, the more he felt love's flame; so greatly did this new fire increase in his heart that he felt himself consumed with love for this beautiful young woman, and he decided that he must have her by whatever means possible.

All he did was in vain, however, for to whatever letters he wrote, to whatever messages he sent, she gave no other reply than that she would keep inviolate her chastity, intending it for the man who would be given to her as her husband. At this the poor lover found himself in a most unhappy state, all the more because he was unable to prevail upon her to keep his letters or his gifts. All the same he was determined to have her, and seeing that her constancy was such that if he wanted to possess her he would have to take her as his wife, he concluded after much inner debate to ask her father for her hand in marriage. And although it seemed to him he was demeaning himself considerably in this, still, knowing that she came of ancient and noble blood, he decided not to put matters off any longer, so great was the love he bore this young woman.

Having thus made up his mind, he sought out a gentleman of Messina with whom he was on familiar terms and related what he had decided, telling him what he wanted him to discuss with Master Lionato. The gentleman went and did as the knight had commissioned him. Master Lionato, when he heard this good news, and knowing well enough the influence and worth of Signor Timbreo, without even seeking further advice from relatives or friends, showed by his gracious reply how pleased he was that the knight deigned to ally himself by marriage with their family. And as soon as he was home he told his wife and Fenicia about the promise he had given to Signor Timbreo. The thing greatly pleased

Fenicia, and with devout heart she thanked our lord God for giving her such a glorious end to her chaste love, and her happiness showed in her face.

But fortune, which never ceases to hinder human happiness in other ways, found a novel way of hindering this marriage so much desired by both parties. Listen and you shall hear how.

Soon it was known all over Messina how in a few days' time Signor Timbreo Cardona was to marry Fenicia, the daughter of Master Lionato. This news generally pleased all the people of Messina, since Master Lionato was a gentleman who made himself much loved—he tried to harm no one and to help everyone as much as he could—so that everyone expressed great happiness at the forthcoming alliance. Now, there was in Messina another young knight of a noble family called Signor Girondo Olerio Valenziano, who had shown himself to be very brave in the war just ended and was moreover one of the most magnificent and bountiful members of the court. This man, hearing the news, was plunged into endless despair, because he had just fallen in love with Fenicia's beauty, and so fiercely did the flames of love lodge in his breast that he firmly believed he would die if he could not have Fenicia for his wife. And having determined to ask her father for her hand in marriage, he thought he would suffer every agony of sorrow when he heard the promise that had been made to Signor Timbreo. When he could find no solace of any kind for his grief, he raved like a madman: conquered by passionate desire and losing all sense of reason, he allowed himself to be carried away into doing a thing unworthy not only of a knight and gentleman but, indeed, of anyone.

Almost always, in all their military undertakings, Signor Girondo had been a companion to Signor Timbreo; between them was a fraternal bond. Concerning this love business, however, for whatever cause, they had hid their feelings from one another. Signor Girondo now hit on the idea of sowing discord between Signor Timbreo and his beloved so that the marriage contract would be broken off. And in this event he himself would ask for her hand in marriage from her father, hoping to have her for the asking. He did not hesitate to put this mad idea into effect. Finding a man suited to his unbridled and blind appetite, he carefully informed him of his scheme. The man whom Signor Girondo had taken to be his confidant and assistant in his crime was a young courtier, a man of poor understanding, better pleased with evil than with good, who, when he had been fully instructed in the plot he was to weave, went the following morning to seek out Signor Timbreo. He found the knight still at home, relaxing all alone in the garden of the inn. As he entered there and was seen approaching, the young man was courteously greeted by Signor Timbreo. After they had exchanged greetings, the young man spoke to Signor Timbreo as follows:

"Signor, I have come at this hour to speak with you on matters of the greatest importance, matters that touch your honor and profit. And since I may speak of certain things that could perhaps offend you, I beg you to pardon me; excuse me for my faithful service, and consider that I do this for a good reason. This much I know: if you are still the noble knight that you have always been, what I am now going to tell you will be of great benefit to you. To come to the point: I must tell you that yesterday I heard how you had met with Master Lionato de' Lionati in order to marry his daughter Fenicia. Beware, signor, what you do, and look to your honor. I say this because a gentleman friend of mine goes almost two or three times a week to lie with her and enjoy her in love; in fact he is going there as usual this evening, and I am going with him as I have on other occasions. If you will give me your word and swear not to vex me or my friend, I will arrange it so that you can see the place and everything else. And, let me add, it's been many months that this friend of mine has been enjoying her. The regard I have for you, and the many favors that you out of your goodness, have done for me, prompt me to make this known to you. Now you must do as seems best to you. To me it is enough to have done my duty in this matter, which my obligation to you required."

At this speech Signor Timbreo was dumbfounded and beside himself, almost indeed out of his senses with emotion. But when he had stood there a good while, a thousand thoughts revolving in his head until bitter and (so it seemed to him) just anger overcame the fervent and loyal love he held for the beautiful Fenicia, he sighed and answered the young man as follows:

"My friend, I can only be eternally obliged to you, seeing how lovingly you care for me and my honor. One day I will show with concrete results how much I am in your debt. For now, I give you all thanks possible. And since you willingly offer to arrange for me to see what I never could have imagined, I pray you, by the love that impelled you to warn me of this fact, go unhesitatingly with your friend. I promise you, on my faith as a true knight, to do no harm to you or him, and to keep this thing a secret always so that your friend can go on enjoying his love in peace. I ought to have been better advised from the first and to have kept my eyes open, inquiring more diligently and minutely into the whole affair."

"Signor," said the young man finally to Signor Timbreo, "this very night, at the third hour, go to the house of Master Lionato, and from those ruined buildings facing out on his garden you will be able to keep watch."

Opposite this hiding place stood the facade of the palazzo of Signor Lionato containing a room of some antiquity at whose windows (open day and night) Fenicia used now and then to appear, because from that side the beauty of the garden might best be enjoyed. Master Lionato and his family, on the other hand, lived in another part of the house, for this palazzo was old and large and roomy enough not only for the household of a gentleman but for the court of a prince.

Now, when everything had been settled on, the deceitful young man went on his way to find the treacherous Girondo, to whom he told all that had been agreed upon with Signor Timbreo Cardona. Signor Girondo was greatly pleased by this, since it seemed to him that his plan was a masterpiece. When the appointed hour arrived, the disloyal Girondo arrayed a servant of his, one whom he had already instructed in what he was to do, in gentlemanly fashion and perfumed him with the sweetest of scents. Then this perfumed servant accompanied the young man who had spoken with Signor Timbreo, while close behind them followed still another man with a ladder on his shoulder.

Who, now, could fully describe Signor Timbreo's state of mind or tell how numerous and how varied were the thoughts that passed through his mind all that day? For my part, I know that I should wear myself out, and all in vain. This overcredulous and unhappy nobleman, blinded with the veil of jealousy, ate next to nothing that day, and anyone who took a look at him would have thought he seemed more dead than alive. Half an hour before the time agreed upon, still thinking it impossible that Fenicia would have given herself as prey to another, he went and hid himself among the ruins in such a way that he could easily see anyone passing by. Then he reflected that young women are fickle, frivolous, giddy, disdainful, and ever hungry for new things. So, damning her one moment and excusing her the next, he waited for any sign of movement.

The night was not very dark, but it was very quiet. Soon he began to be aware of approaching footsteps and some indistinct conversation. Then he saw three men passing by and recognized clearly the young man who had warned him that morning, but the other two he was unable to identify. As the three passed before him he heard what the perfumed man, dressed like a lover, was saying to the one carrying the ladder: "See that you place the ladder carefully at the window without making any noise, because, when we were last here, the Signorina Fenicia told me that you had leaned it there too noisily. Do everything neatly and quietly."

Signor Timbreo heard clearly these words that were as sharp and piercing as kitchen spits in his heart. And although he was alone and had no weapon but his sword—whereas the passers-by were armed with lances in addition to their swords and probably wore armor to boot—so great and so pungent was the jealousy gnawing at his heart and so intense the wrath that inflamed him that he was close to rushing out of his hiding place and making a deadly assault, intending either to kill the one whom he judged to be the lover of Fenicia or else, by being slain, to end right then and there the heartache and excessive grief that he wretchedly suffered. But remembering the promise he had given, and believing that it would be extremely craven and villainous to attack those to whom he had given his word, filled with anger and vexation and wrath and fury, champing at the bit, he waited to see how it would come out.

The three men, arriving below the window of Master Lionato's house on that side we spoke of before, leaned the ladder very gently against the balcony, and the one who took the part of the lover climbed up and went into the house, as though he had an assignation within. When the disconsolate Signor Timbreo saw this, believing firmly that he who had climbed up had gone in to lie with Fenicia, he was assailed with the most intense grief imaginable and thought he was going to faint away. But so powerfully did his just anger (as it seemed to him) work in him that it chased away all jealousy. The fervent and sincere love he bore for Fenicia not only froze completely but turned into cruel hate. And so, not wanting to wait until his rival came out of the house, he left from the place where he had been hiding and went back to his inn.

The young man, who had seen him leave and who clearly recognized him, rightly guessed what the effect on him had been. And so, not long afterward he made a signal, and the servant who had climbed up came back down, and they went together to the house of Signor Girondo and told him the whole thing. He rejoiced at this and already began to think of himself as the possessor of the beautiful Fenicia.

Signor Timbreo, having slept little for the rest of the night, got up early and summoned the Messinese citizen who had served as his intermediary in seeking the hand in marriage of Fenicia from her father, and told him what he wanted him to do. The Messinese citizen, fully informed of the mind and will of Signor Timbreo, went at dinnertime to find Master Lionato, whom he found pacing up and down in the dining room waiting for dinner to be served, while Fenicia, also there, embroidered some work of silk in the company of her two younger sisters and her mother. When the Messinese citizen had arrived and had been graciously welcomed by Master Lionato, he said as follows: "Master Lionato, I have a message for you, and your wife and Fenicia as well, from Signor Timbreo." "You are welcome," replied Master Lionato. "What is it? Wife, and you, too, Fenicia, come hear with me what Signor Timbreo has to say to us." The emissary spoke in this manner: "It is often said that an envoy relating merely what is imposed on him ought not to suffer any penalty for doing so. I come to you sent by another person, and it grieves me infinitely to bring you news that must annoy you. Signor Timbreo di Cardona sends word to you, Master Lionato, and to your wife, that you should provide yourselves with another son-in-law, because he does not intend to have you for his in-laws—certainly not through any failing on the part of yourselves, whom he believes in and considers to be loyal and good, but because he has seen with his own eyes something in Fenicia that he would never have believed otherwise. And so he leaves it to you to provide for your own affairs as you wish. Now, to you, Fenicia, he says that the love he bore you ought never to have received the reward you have given him, and that you ought to provide yourself another husband in just the same way that you have taken another lover. You ought in fact to take the very man to whom you have given your virginity. He, Signor Timbreo, intends to have nothing further to do with you as one who will surely cuckold her husband."

Fenicia, hearing this bitter and vituperative message, was stricken as though dead. So were Master Lionato and his wife. Nevertheless, when he had regained life and breath, which almost failed him in his astonishment, Master Lionato spoke to the emissary as follows: "My friend, I always feared, from the very first time you spoke to me of this marriage, that Signor Timbreo would not hold steady in his request, since I knew then as I know now that I am a poor gentleman and not his social equal. Even so, it seems to me that, if he was having second thoughts about taking her as his wife, it would have been enough for him to say he didn't want her any more, rather than inflicting such a vindictive stain on her with this label of whore. True enough, anything is possible, but I know how my daughter has been brought up and what her habits are. Someday, I firmly believe, God in his great justice will cause the truth to be known."

When this answer had been given, the Messinese citizen went on his way. Master Lionato continued to hold to the opinion that Signor Timbreo had changed his mind about the marital alliance because he was debasing himself too much and falling off from his ancestors. The lineage of Master Lionato was in fact venerable and noble and highly regarded in Messina, but his wealth was only that of a private gentleman, even though ancient records proved that his forefathers had owned much land and many castles with wide-ranging jurisdiction. But through vicissitudes in the island's history and through civil war their seigniories had decayed, as one sees in other families as well. And so now the good father, never having discovered the least behavior in his daughter that was not chaste, concluded simply that the knight disdained their poverty and present lack of good fortune.

For her part, Fenicia, to whom any mishaps brought extreme sorrow and faintness of heart, hearing herself accused of a such a terrible wrong and being a tender and delicate young woman not accustomed to the blows of hostile fortune, abandoned herself to despair, wishing more for death than for life. And so, afflicted by the most profound and penetrating of sorrows, she sank down as though dead and, suddenly losing all the color in her complexion, resembled more a marble statue than a living creature. She was picked up and carried to bed, where, with warm clothes and other remedies, her fallen spirits were recalled to her in short order. And when they sent for the doctor, the news spread through all Messina that Fenicia, the daughter of Master Lionato, was so gravely ill that her life was in danger. When they heard this news, many gentle ladies, relatives and friends, came to visit the disconsolate Fenicia, and when they understood the occasion of her sickness, they busied themselves as best they could to comfort her. And as usually happens when lots of ladies are involved, they said different things about this piteous affair but generally agreed in rebuking Signor Timbreo with bitter censure.

The greater part of them were around the bed of the sick young lady when Fenicia, having perfectly understood what they had been saying, caught her breath as best she could and, seeing that for pity of her nearly all of them were in tears, in a weak voice begged them all to be silent. Then she faintly spoke as follows:

[Fenicia urges them to accept God's will, complaining not against the fact of her repudiation but rather the manner in which it was done, and asserting the dignity of her family. She wonders if perhaps God has done this to spare her the pride and arrogance that might have come through her elevation to such a high social station through the marriage. She prays that God may open Signor Timbreo's eyes, not so that she can marry him but so that her reputation can be cleared. She knows that she is innocent in the eyes of God, to whom she commends her soul. Thereupon Fenicia is so stricken that her doctors give her up for lost and she is mourned by her distraught family.]

Five or six hours passed by, and the order was given for Fenicia's burial on the following day. When the throng of ladies had left, her mother, more dead than alive, kept a relative with her—the wife of a brother of Master Lionato—and the two of them together, not wanting to have anyone else with them, ordered water to be put on the fire and shut themselves up in the room, where, undressing Fenicia, they began to wash her with warm water. The bewildered vital spirits of Fenicia, having taken a walk for some seven hours or so, returned to their proper function when her cold limbs were being washed. Giving manifest signs that she was alive, the young woman began to open her eyes a little. The mother and her sister-in-law nearly cried out in astonishment. But taking courage they put their hands against her heart and felt it give some movement. At this they were firmly convinced that the young woman was alive. And so, with warm clothes and other inducements, without making any noise, they brought Fenicia to the point of being almost completely herself again. Opening her eyes, she said with a deep sigh, "Alas, where am I?" "Don't you see," said her mother, "that you are here with me and your aunt? Such a deep swoon came upon you that we thought you were dead, but, God be praised, you are alive." "Ah, how much better it would be," answered Fenicia, "if I were dead indeed and free of my worries!" "My daughter," said her mother and her aunt, "you must live, since it pleases God, and he will provide a remedy for all things."

At this the mother, hiding the joy she felt, opened a door of the room a little and sent for Master Lionato, who came right away. There is no need to ask if he was happy when he saw his daughter restored to herself. Turning over many things in his mind, he decided first of all that no one should know of this matter, choosing instead to send the young woman out of Messina to the villa of the very brother whose wife was then with them. And so, when they had restored the young woman with delicacies to eat and costly wine, and when she had gotten back her former beauty and strength, he sent for his brother and instructed him fully in what he wanted him to do. The arrangement they made was as follows: Master Girolamo (such was the name of the brother of Master Lionato) was to conduct Fenicia on the following night to his own house and there keep her in secrecy in the company of his wife. And then, when he had provided what was necessary in his villa, early one morning Master Girolamo sent his wife there with Fenicia, along with one of his own daughters and one of Fenicia's sisters, she being thirteen or fourteen years old, whereas Fenicia was sixteen. He did this so that when Fenicia had grown older and had changed in appearance, as happens with maturation, he might then in two or three years marry her off under another name.

[Master Lionato orders a funeral suited to his daughter's rank, buries her coffin with ceremony, and emblazons on her stone monument an epitaph lamenting her cruel fate and protesting her innocence. Signor Timbreo soon begins to have second thoughts, wondering if the man he witnessed might have entered the window to see some other lover. Signor Girondo too is smitten in conscience. Asking Signor Timbreo to come with him to the church where Fenicia's tomb is placed, Signor Girondo admits what he has done and begs to be killed for his crimes. His confession elicits instead a tearful pardon from Signor Timbreo and a request for assistance in doing everything possible to restore Fenicia's good name. The remorse of the two knights in the presence of Master Lionato wins his pardon in turn, and he requests that Signor Timbreo agree to marry a lady of Master Lionato's choosing so long as she is pleasing to Signor Timbreo. Fenicia, still in concealment, is glad to learn of this agreement and of her recovered reputation.

Even though all seems well now, a year or more is allowed to pass, during which time Fenicia grows more and more beautiful. Her sister Belfiore also flowers into womanhood. Escorted at last to the country villa by Master Lionato, the two knights are struck by the young ladies' beauty. Signor Timbreo does not recognize Fenicia, who is presented to

him by the name of Lucilla, though a vague stirring in his
heart reminds him of Fenicia and increases his love for this
lady. He marries her, and at the wedding feast expresses
once more his remorse and sense of loss for what he has
done. The revelation of Fenicia's identity is the reward for
his constancy and devotion. Signor Girondo begs forgiveness anew, is welcomed into the happy group, and success-
fully pleads for the hand of Belfiore. A double wedding
ensues in which Signor Timbreo, having wedded "Lucilla,"
is now bound in matrimony to his Fenicia. They all prepare
to return to Messina, where they are honored by the court
of King Piero and his queen and are given a handsome set-
tlement. Master Lionato profits, too, from the royal bounty.]

La Prima Parte de le Novelle del Bandello was first published in Lucca in
1554. This new translation is based on that edition.

Further Reading

Berger, Harry, Jr. "Against the Sink-a-Pace: Sexual and Family Politics in *Much Ado About Nothing*." *Shakespeare Quarterly* 33 (1982): 302–313. Berger explores the social values and practices that generate both Hero's near-tragedy and Beatrice's wariness of marriage. Males in the play are unable to free themselves of the patriarchal and mysogynist "assumptions of their community," and, accordingly, the comic resolution is unable to resolve convincingly the social tensions and contradictions that have become articulate.

Berry, Ralph. "Problems of Knowing." *Shakespeare's Comedies: Explorations in Form*. Princeton, N.J.: Princeton Univ. Press, 1972. Berry finds a unifying principle for the play's three plots in their common concern with "the limits and methods of knowledge." The verb "to know" occurs with striking frequency in the play, and its action and emotion emerge from the fact that characters are denied reliable means of knowing, depending rather upon the unreliable evidence of eye and ear.

Cook, Carol. " 'The Sign and Semblance of Her Honor': Reading Gender Difference in *Much Ado About Nothing*." *PMLA* 101 (1986): 186–202. Reading the "merry war" between Beatrice and Benedick as a symptom of the sexual conflicts of Messina, Cook finds that the play's ending in multiple marriages leaves conspicuously unresolved the social and psychological tensions that are revealed by the anxious joking about cuckoldry and indeed in the very plot of a young man too easily persuaded that his lady is unfaithful to him and who can be regenerated and forgiven only after he thinks that he has caused her death.

Evans, Bertrand. *Shakespeare's Comedies*, pp. 68–87. Oxford: Clarendon Press, 1960. Evans patiently traces the play's witty exploitation of the different levels of awareness among characters and the audience. The play is structured around eight "practices," or plots, which are designed to lead characters into error but which finally are resolved in the play's "joyful close."

Fergusson, Francis. *"The Comedy of Errors* and *Much Ado*

About Nothing." Sewanee Review 62 (1954): 24–37. Rpt. in *The Human Image in Dramatic Literature.* Garden City, N.Y.: Doubleday, 1957; Gloucester, Mass.: P. Smith, 1969. Rpt. also in *Shakespeare's Comedies: An Anthology of Modern Criticism,* ed. Laurence Lerner. Harmondsworth and Baltimore: Penguin, 1967; and in *Discussions of Shakespeare's Romantic Comedy,* ed. Herbert Weil, Jr. Boston: D. C. Heath, 1966. Fergusson uses *Much Ado* to explore the nature of laughter and comedy itself. He compares the play to the farce of *The Comedy of Errors,* and finds that *Much Ado* extends and deepens the comedy of mistaken identities of the earlier play through its richer poetic texture and festive form.

Hays, Janice. "Those 'Soft and Delicate Desires': *Much Ado* and the Distrust of Women." In *The Woman's Part: Feminist Criticism of Shakespeare,* ed. Carolyn Ruth Swift Lenz, Gayle Greene, and Carol Thomas Neely. Urbana, Ill.: Univ. of Illinois Press, 1980. For Hays, the Hero-Claudio plot is a "ritual action" in which male fear and distrust of women is articulated and purged. Claudio must learn to move beyond his anxieties to trust and to be trustworthy, and the action works to develop his willingness to open up to emotional possibilities that his self-centeredness has denied him.

Hunter, Robert Grams. *"Much Ado About Nothing." Shakespeare and the Comedy of Forgiveness.* New York and London: Columbia Univ. Press, 1965. For Hunter, *Much Ado* is the first of Shakespeare's comedies of forgiveness, revealing the paradigmatic Christian pattern of sin/contrition/forgiveness. Claudio's sin is the failure to "trust love absolutely." He comes, however, to recognize his error, and the play allows an audience, like Messinan society, to forgive him, seeing him as "an image of its own frailty."

Jorgensen, Paul A. "Much Ado About *Nothing." Redeeming Shakespeare's Words.* Berkeley and Los Angeles: Univ. of California Press, 1962. In an essay exploring the rich significations of the word "nothing" available to Elizabethans, Jorgensen examines a number of Shakespearean uses of the word, including its appearance in the play's title.

Kirsch, Arthur. *"Much Ado About Nothing." Shakespeare*

and the Experience of Love. Cambridge: Cambridge Univ. Press, 1981. Kirsch uses the insights of Freudian psychology and Christian theology to explore the comedy's presentation of the "problems of narcissism." Its three plots, linked, he sees, by "analogies of action and language," demonstrate the possibilities of transcending shallow egotism in a comic triumph of humor, faith, and love.

Leggatt, Alexander. *"Much Ado About Nothing." Shakespeare's Comedy of Love*. London: Methuen; New York: Barnes and Noble, 1974. In the "interplay of formality and naturalism," Leggatt discovers a unity in the play's two romantic plots that serves to complicate the easy antithesis between them that many have seen. The Hero-Claudio plot in its very conventionality is rooted in the "familiar rhythms of life"; the Beatrice-Benedick plot, for all its richly individualized character, is finally seen "as a matter of convention."

Levin, Richard A. "Crime and Cover-up in Messina." *Love and Society in Shakespearean Comedy: A Study of Dramatic Form and Content*. Newark, Del.: Univ. of Delaware Press, 1985. Finding the play's comic action darkened by the unacknowledged anxieties and insecurities of characters in the romantic plots, Levin focuses on the social tensions and contradictions revealed within the world of Messina. The comedy's happy end is achieved only by attributing all malice to Don John and by a too-eager acceptance of the characters' perfunctory repentance.

Nevo, Ruth. "Better than Reportingly." *Comic Transformations in Shakespeare*. London: Methuen, 1980. Nevo examines the "equilibrium" established between the play's two romantic plots. In each, deception works to make manifest what has been "latent," and each transforms its participants to meet the demands of the conventions of both comedy and marriage.

Ormerod, David. "Faith and Fashion in *Much Ado About Nothing*." *Shakespeare Survey* 25 (1972): 93–105. Ormerod structures his reading of the play around the opposition of "faith" and "fashion." Faith, identified with the mythological figure of Hercules, is the emotional and spiritual condition that resists appearances and makes love possible, but fashion, identified with the blind Cupid, is the commitment to the world of deceptive senses that destroys and "deforms."

Ornstein, Robert. *"Much Ado About Nothing." Shakespeare's Comedies: From Roman Farce to Romantic Mystery*. Newark, Del.: Univ. of Delaware Press, 1986. Ornstein finds in the interrelatedness of its two plots that the play asserts the moral primacy of an "unassuming decency" over the "moral superiority that leads to contempt." The comic ending celebrates the triumph of trust over faithlessness, but "nothing that is painful is forgotten": the wedding scene necessarily reminds us of the agonies of the aborted wedding earlier.

Prouty, Charles Tyler. *The Sources of "Much Ado About Nothing."* New Haven, Conn.: Yale Univ. Press, 1950. Examining the source material and its relation to Shakespeare's play, Prouty traces the connections between the two romantic plots and considers the nature of the main plot, especially the character of Claudio. In addition, he provides a text of Peter Beverley's *History of Ariodanto and Genevra* (1566), an English adaptation of the story from Ariosto's *Orlando Furioso*, which serves as the ultimate source of the Hero-Claudio plot.

Rossiter, A. P. *"Much Ado About Nothing."* In *Angel with Horns and Other Shakespeare Lectures*, ed. Graham Storey. London: Longmans, Green, 1961. Rpt. in *Shakespeare, The Comedies: A Collection of Critical Essays*, ed. Kenneth Muir. Englewood Cliffs, N.J.: Prentice-Hall, 1965. Rossiter attempts to account for the highly wrought wit of *Much Ado*, which he finds as much in the interrelatedness of the plots as in the inventiveness of the language. Language and structure emerge from the play's concern with misapprehension and misprision; the play is a comedy of mistaken identities in which, above all, characters mistake their own natures and needs.

Siegel, Paul N. "The Turns of the Dance: An Essay on *Much Ado About Nothing.*" *Shakespeare in His Time and Ours*. Notre Dame, Ind.: Univ. of Notre Dame Press, 1968. Siegel traces the parallels between and the patterning of the two romantic plots. Beatrice and Benedick repeat with significant variations the actions of Hero and Claudio; the couples are united only at the end in the dance that confirms and celebrates the comic ending.

Memorable Lines

How much better is it to weep at joy than to joy at weeping!
(LEONATO   1.1.27–28)

He wears his faith but as the fashion of his hat.
(BEATRICE   1.1.70–71)

I see, lady, the gentleman is not in your books.
(MESSENGER   1.1.73–74)

BENEDICK   What, my dear Lady Disdain! Are you yet living?
BEATRICE   Is it possible disdain should die while she hath
such meet food to feed it as Signor Benedick?
(1.1.113–116)

. . . as merry as the day is long.   (BEATRICE   2.1.46)

Speak low, if you speak love.   (DON PEDRO   2.1.93)

Friendship is constant in all other things
Save in the office and affairs of love.
(CLAUDIO   2.1.169–170)

It keeps on the windy side of care.
(BEATRICE   2.1.299–300)

Rich she shall be, that's certain; wise, or I'll none; virtuous,
or I'll never cheapen her; fair, or I'll never look on her; mild,
or come not near me; noble, or not I for an angel; of good
discourse, an excellent musician, and her hair shall be of
what color it please God.   (BENEDICK   2.3.29–33)

[*Song*]   Sigh no more, ladies, sigh no more.
Men were deceivers ever.   (BALTHASAR   2.3.61–62)

Sits the wind in that corner?   (BENEDICK   2.3.101–102)

Contempt, farewell, and maiden pride, adieu!
(BEATRICE   3.1.109)

To be well-favored man is the gift of fortune, but to write and read comes by nature.   (DOGBERRY   3.3.15–16)

They that touch pitch will be defiled.   (DOGBERRY   3.3.56)

The fashion wears out more apparel than the man.
                                               (CONRADE   3.3.138–139)

If I were as tedious as a king, I could find in my heart to bestow it all of your worship.   (DOGBERRY   3.5.20–21)

O, what men dare do! What men may do! What men daily do, not knowing what they do!   (CLAUDIO   4.1.18–19)

O, that I had been writ down an ass!   (DOGBERRY   4.2.86)

For there was never yet philosopher
That could endure the toothache patiently.
                                               (LEONATO   5.1.35–36)

What though care killed a cat, thou hast mettle enough in thee to kill care.   (CLAUDIO   5.1.133–134)

I was not born under a rhyming planet.
                                               (BENEDICK   5.2.39–40)

Contributors

DAVID BEVINGTON, Phyllis Fay Horton Professor of Humanities at the University of Chicago, is editor of *The Complete Works of Shakespeare* (Scott, Foresman, 1980) and of *Medieval Drama* (Houghton Mifflin, 1975). His latest critical study is *Action Is Eloquence: Shakespeare's Language of Gesture* (Harvard University Press, 1984).

DAVID SCOTT KASTAN, Professor of English and Comparative Literature at Columbia University, is the author of *Shakespeare and the Shapes of Time* (University Press of New England, 1982).

JAMES HAMMERSMITH, Associate Professor of English at Auburn University, has published essays on various facets of Renaissance drama, including literary criticism, textual criticism, and printing history.

ROBERT KEAN TURNER, Professor of English at the University of Wisconsin–Milwaukee, is a general editor of the New Variorum Shakespeare (Modern Language Association of America) and a contributing editor to *The Dramatic Works in the Beaumont and Fletcher Canon* (Cambridge University Press, 1966–).

JAMES SHAPIRO, who coedited the bibliographies with David Scott Kastan, is Assistant Professor of English at Columbia University.

✢

JOSEPH PAPP, one of the most important forces in theater today, is the founder and producer of the New York Shakespeare Festival, America's largest and most prolific theatrical institution. Since 1954 Mr. Papp has produced or directed all but one of Shakespeare's plays—in Central Park, in schools, off and on Broadway, and at the Festival's permanent home, The Public Theater. He has also produced such award-winning plays and musical works as *Hair, A Chorus Line, Plenty,* and *The Mystery of Edwin Drood,* among many others.

Shakespeare
ALIVE!

☐ 27081-8 $4.50/$5.50 in Canada

From Joseph Papp, America's foremost theater producer, and writer Elizabeth Kirkland: a captivating tour through the world of William Shakespeare.

Discover the London of Shakespeare's time, a fascinating place to be—full of mayhem and magic, exploration and exploitation, courtiers and foreigners. Stroll through narrow, winding streets crowded with merchants and minstrels, hoist a pint in a rowdy alehouse, and hurry across the river to the open-air Globe Theatre to the latest play written by a young man named Will Shakespeare.

SHAKESPEARE ALIVE! spirits you back to the very heart of that London—as everyday people might have experienced it. Find out how young people fell in love, how workers and artists made ends meet, what people found funny and what they feared most. Go on location with an Elizabethan theater company, learn how plays were produced, where Shakespeare's plots came from and how he transformed them. Hear the music of Shakespeare's language and the words we still use today that were first spoken in his time.

Open this book and elbow your way into the Globe with the groundlings. You'll be joining one of the most democratic audiences the theater has ever known—alewives, apprentices, shoemakers and nobles—in applauding the dazzling wordplay and swordplay brought to you by William Shakespeare.

Look for **SHAKESPEARE ALIVE!** at your local bookstore or use the coupon below:

Bantam is proud to announce an important new edition of:

The Complete Works Of William Shakespeare

Featuring:

*The complete texts with modern spelling and punctuation

*Vivid, readable introductions by noted Shakespearean scholar David Bevington

*New forewords by Joseph Papp, renowned producer, director, and founder of the New York Shakespeare Festival

*Stunning, original cover art by Mark English, the most awarded illustrator in the history of the Society of Illustrators

*Photographs from some of the most celebrated performances by the New York Shakespeare Festival

*Complete source materials, notes, and annotated bibliographies based on the latest scholarships

*Stage histories for each play

ACCESSIBLE * AUTHORITATIVE * COMPLETE

SHAKESPEARE
The Complete works in 29 Volumes

Bantam Drama Classics

☐	21279	Sophocles: Complete Plays	$3.25
☐	21219	Euripides: Ten Plays	$3.50
☐	21261	Aristophanes: Complete Plays	$3.95
☐	21280	Henrik Ibsen: Four Great Plays	$2.95
☐	21118	Rostand: Cyrano De Bergerac	$1.75
☐	21211	Anton Chekhov: Five Major Plays	$2.95

Buy them at your local bookstore or use this handy coupon for ordering:

Bantam Books, Dept. CL5, 414 East Golf Road,
Des Plaines, IL 60016

Please send me the books I have checked above. I am enclosing
$_____ (Please add $1.50 to cover postage and handling.)
Send check or money order—no cash or C.O.D.s please.

Mr/Ms _____

Address _____

City/State _____ Zip _____

CL5—2/88

Please allow four to six weeks for delivery. This offer expires
8/88. Prices and availability subject to change without notice.

BANTAM
SHOP·AT·HOME
C·A·T·A·L·O·G

Special Offer
Buy a Bantam Book
for only 50¢.

Now you can have Bantam's catalog filled with hundreds of titles plus take advantage of our unique and exciting bonus book offer. A special offer which gives you the opportunity to purchase a Bantam book for only 50¢. Here's how!

By ordering any five books at the regular price per order, you can also choose any other single book listed (up to a $5.95 value) for just 50¢. Some restrictions do apply, but for further details why not send for Bantam's catalog of titles today!

Just send us your name and address and we will send you a catalog!